Deep South

Deep South

Memory
and
Observation

Erskine Caldwell

Foreword by
Guy Owen

Brown Thrasher Books
The University of Georgia Press
Athens and London

95-034138

Published in 1995 as a Brown Thrasher Book
by the University of Georgia Press, Athens, Georgia 30602
© 1966, 1968 by Erskine Caldwell
Foreword to the Brown Thrasher Edition
© 1980 by the University of Georgia Press

All rights reserved

The paper in this book meets the guidelines for
permanence and durability of the Committee on
Production Guidelines for Book Longevity of the
Council on Library Resources.

Printed in the United States of America

99   98   97   96   95   P   5   4   3   2   1

Library of Congress Cataloging in Publication Data
Caldwell, Erskine, 1903–
Deep South : memory and observation / Erskine Caldwell ;
foreword by Guy Owen.
p.   cm.
"Part 1 of Deep South was first published in England under the
title In the shadow of the steeple."
Originally published: New York : Weybright and Talley, 1968.
"Brown Thrasher books."
ISBN 0-8203-1716-0 (pbk. : alk. paper)
1. Protestant churches—Southern States. 2. Southern States—
Religion. 3. Caldwell, Erskine, 1903– —Homes and haunts—Southern
States. 1. Caldwell, Erskine, 1903– In the shadow of the steeple. 11. Title.
BR535.C29 1995
280′.4′09750904—dc20   94-36671

British Library Cataloging in Publication Data available

Part 1 of *Deep South* was first published in England in 1966
under the title *In the Shadow of the Steeple*.

Contents

CENTRAL ARKANSAS LIBRARY SYSTEM
ROOSEVELT L. THOMPSON BRANCH LIBRARY
LITTLE ROCK, ARKANSAS

GEORGIA INSTITUTE OF TECH LIBRARY
PRICE $00.00
DATE 00-00-00
GIFT OF PERSONAL COPY

Foreword

WHEN ERSKINE CALDWELL published *Deep South*, the
story of his encounters with the varieties of Protestantism, he was almost two generations beyond the crest of
fame that followed *Tobacco Road* and *God's Little Acre*.
As a result, though it is his best nonfiction treatment of
his native region, the book received little attention and
did not reach the wide audience it deserved—no doubt
sufficient reason for reissuing it now. Incidentally, I
prefer the title of the earlier—and shorter—English edition, *Under the Shadow of the Steeple*, because it suggests
the boundaries of his subject, as well as the author's
ironic tone. By the time of the civil rights movement
Caldwell had become convinced that the church cast a
sinister shadow across the rural and small-town South.

The reader should not expect a balanced and objective
history of Protestantism below the Mason-Dixon line.
Caldwell, like most southern novelists, cares almost
nothing for abstractions or dry theories. He pays only
lip service to his announced thesis: to examine the practices of the Protestant church of the 1920s and 1960s in
order "to illuminate to some degree the churchly life of
the two eras of the Deep South." One can almost hear
the author's sigh of relief once he has hammered this
out; now he can get down to the writing that he does

best, no doubt adding a pinch of fiction here and there.

As in his other books of reportage, this one is enlivened with some marvelous vignettes and yarns that, with a few revisions, would fit into a collection of his best stories. Like his strongest fiction, they leave a vibrant and haunting after-image. One can easily lift them out and give them titles: "Mr. Goldstein and the Two-Dollar Shoes," "The Preacher and the Prostitute," "Father Plays Detective," or "The Preacher and the Moonshiner." There is also the comic folk tale (a Caldwell signature), "The Knife Swappers of Cumberland," as well as the tragic "The Peg-legged Minister and the Burning Church" and "The Death of Moses Coffee," two memorable narratives added to the 1968 edition.

Caldwell is preeminently a novelist, so it should not be surprising that *Deep South*, crammed as it is with yarns and interviews, can be read like an episodic novel, with the author's father, Ira Sylvester, as the protagonist. The suspense centers around why he decided to become a minister and how long he will remain an A.R.P. troubleshooter. The climax comes when he repudiates the church to pursue a career in education.

A quietly heroic pastor, first introduced in Caldwell's autobiography, *Call It Experience*, Ira Sylvester is well worth meeting and knowing. Certainly his warm presence makes this one of Caldwell's most pleasant books, in spite of all the other grotesques. No doubt idealized, he seems larger than life when contrasted with the stunted, twisted souls around him. His love for his son is as clear as his religious vocation is blurred. One comes to know him as one never quite knows Jeeter Lester or Ty Ty Walden, or the oppressive gallery of failed ministers in Caldwell's "cyclorama of the South." Shining like a halo are his empathy and compassion (like his son's) for the underdog: defenseless women and Blacks, the exploited poor. His charity, gentleness, intelligence, unflappable sense of humor—in sum, his unimpeachable humanity—are clearly and lovingly rendered. Caldwell's message is unambiguous though unstated: if the church had more dedicated leaders like Ira Sylvester, it would be an indispensable institution, one effecting needed social changes rather than impeding them.

One feels that the author was exceedingly lucky in his father, as Caldwell admits. Certainly a budding novelist would not ask for a better education for the writing profession than his early exposure to a wide spectrum of interesting characters, from moonshiners to con-men evangelists, and such a variety of locales. Little wonder that he has written more about religion in fiction than any of his fellow novelists.

The style of *Deep South* is recognizably Caldwellian, though more complex and varied than that of *Tobacco Road*, since the people are, by and large, more complex. There is the inevitable sharp eye for details, the subdued poetry, the reliance on words from Anglo-Saxon roots, the habitual trick of repetition, the pervasive irony—which becomes Swiftian at times. It is a flexible style, lucid and serviceable; above all, fluid and readable. It does not get between the reader and the message; instead it leaves him with a series of evocative images and scenes:

Along the trails and footpaths in the ravines, out of sight of paved roads and highways, shacks and cabins tilt and sag and rot on the verge of collapse in the shadow of the green summer thatch of white oaks and black walnuts. The faces of the old people are saying that all is lost and tomorrow will be like yesterday and today—unless it is worse.

This is more than a description of a particular landscape;

it suggests the author's attitude toward religion and life in the rural South.

Looking back over his long career, one can follow Caldwell's compelling interest in religion—especially its more bizarre manifestations—which culminates in *Deep South*. In his first published essay, "The Georgia Cracker" (1926), he attacks boosters and demagogues, but over half of the satire is spent censuring "bogus religionists." He continued his attack in *You Have Seen Their Faces* (1935): "The failure of the church to preach its own convictions in the sharecropper country has resulted in its becoming a burlesque of religion." Religious services, he contends, serve mainly a social purpose or as an emotional outlet. Christian ideals are seldom transmuted into ethical conduct, always the test for Caldwell, as it was for his father. From Sister Bessie to the satanic Semon Dye of *Journeyman*, Caldwell has been fascinated by the horrible and the comic elements of bush religions. He is obviously haunted by the scenes he early witnessed of snake-handlers, glossolalia, and bloodletting; yet he is shrewd enough to note that such experiences, if not of genuine transcendence, are narcotic for impoverished and ignorant sharecroppers and millworkers. As *Journeyman* makes clear, their lives would be emptier without them—even when they are duped and victimized by trickster evangelists.

Yet Caldwell observes the comedy, too, in the circus-like revivals, the theatrical posturing, the competition of testifiers to come up with interesting sins to confess, the implications of sex in the sermons, and emotional writhings that make a revival service—again, as in *Journeyman*—akin to pornography. As the born-again preacher from the Cumberlands reveals, "Folks like to listen to me preach. They like

[x

to hear about lying and fornicating and stealing the way I talk about it."

A bleak picture of the failure of modern Protestantism viewed by a disillusioned minister's son. Yet snake-handling and nigger-baiting are not the whole picture, and Caldwell is honest enough to admit it. He acknowledges that there are many moderate Methodists and Baptists with progressive ideas who have never fondled a rattlesnake nor burned a cross. Furthermore, he obviously approves of the brand of Protestantism practiced by Blacks, even when it is hopelessly emotional, no doubt because it depends little on theology and does not foster hatred and violence. Surprisingly, after all the depressing evidence for the failure of the "churchly life," Caldwell concludes on a note of optimism, absent from the English edition of the book. He allows a mulatto to speak for him, a churchgoer who is proud of *both* his black and white heritage. This is all the more an affirmation when you know that Caldwell believed that the hope of the South was integration through intermarriage, as he dramatized in the mulatto "Christ-child" of *Place Called Estherville*.

Erskine Caldwell has been too long neglected by his native state and the South. (He is far more widely accepted in France and Russia.) At a time when a Niagara of books floods the country on minor writers and one-book authors, there is no biography or full-length study of this masterful storyteller whom William Faulkner ranked among our half-dozen greatest novelists. It is time amends were made: let this new edition of *Deep South* be a beginning.

GUY OWEN

In the Shadow
of the Steeple

One

BEING A MINISTER'S SON in the Deep South in the early years of the twentieth century and growing up in a predominantly religious environment was my good fortune in life.

The experience of living for six months or a year or sometimes longer in one Southern state after another, in cities and small towns and countrysides, and being exposed to numerous varieties of Protestant sects which were Calvinist in doctrine and fundamentalist in practice proved to be of more value to me than the intermittent and frequently-curtailed secular education I received during the first seventeen years of my life.

This fortunate destiny of birth and circumstance could otherwise have been tragic and unrewarding if both my mother and my father had not been wise and tolerant and, consequently, made it possible for me to seek an understanding of life beyond the confines prescribed by prevailing religious beliefs and prejudiced attitudes of mind.

My father was the Reverend Ira Sylvester Caldwell, a North Carolinian, an Associate Reformed Presbyterian ordained minister, a veteran of the Spanish–American War, and a graduate of Erskine College, Erskine Theological Seminary, and the University of Georgia. My mother, Caroline Bell Caldwell, was a Virginian, a teacher, and a graduate of Mary Baldwin College and the University of Georgia. I had neither a brother nor a sister.

Until I was twelve years old, I called my father Bud and my mother was Tarrie. My name for my mother had been derived at an early age from Carrie, which I had been constantly hearing as a diminutive of Caroline. Likewise, by that time, Bud had come to sound to me as befitting and authentic as my own name. Neither parent at any time had ever asked or demanded of me that I call them by names other than Bud and Tarrie.

Aside from the customary formal title of Reverend, my father was known to many of his acquaintances as Ira. In the informal atmosphere of barbershops and on fishing trips with friends it was not unusual for him to be called Preacher.

However, my father's brothers and sisters and other relatives always called him Bud, probably because he was the elder of his parents' six children. Feeling just as closely related to him as anyone else, it had always seemed to me the natural thing to call him Bud, too.

As it happened, though, on my twelfth birthday one of my aunts said it was shocking and disrespectful for me to call my parents Bud and Tarrie, and I was coerced and bribed to promise never again to call them by those names. The bribe I received was a glossy blue bicycle with a bell on the handle-bar and a tyre pump clamped to the frame. I soon became accustomed to saying Mother or *Mère* instead of Tarrie but, while not forgetting the promise I had made, I was never able to think of my father actually having the name Father or *Père*.

There was never a discussion about what I was to call my father instead of Bud but, as if we had found a compromise and had entered into a secret agreement, there-

[2

after when we were together and no other person was present, my name for him was either Ira Sylvester or I.S. We considered this to be a personal matter concerning us alone and therefore did not think of it as being a breach of promise. After all, even though my aunt may have assumed that I would call him by no name other than Father or *Père*, or perhaps Papa or Dad, the only promise I had made was never again to call him Bud.

My father never objected even in later years to my calling him either Ira Sylvester or I.S. and, when I saw him look at me with a blinking of his eyes and an unmistakable smile, it was as if my aunt had never offered to give me a bicycle. However, he undoubtedly realized that it was inevitable that a boy at my age who wanted a bicycle as much as I did would promise anything within reason in order to have one.

It was during this time that I began to be curious about what connection there was between my father and religion. Perhaps it was because he was darkly tall and muscular and always wore starched white shirts and a slightly-askew black bow necktie with his dark suits that he had the appearance of a dignified clergyman. Also, I knew he preached in churches and travelled frequently for religious purposes. However, I did not know why he was a minister and how it had happened that he became one.

When I asked him to tell me the reason for his entering the ministry instead of being a doctor or lawyer or storekeeper, he was evasive and had little to say, probably thinking I was not old enough then to understand a full explanation. The only thing Ira Sylvester would tell me was that he had studied for the ministry because his mother had asked him to do so.

It was not until many years later that I found out the reason why his mother had asked him to become a minister.

At the time I was twelve years old my knowledge of religion and the evidence of its emotional appeal was confined to what I had heard and seen within only the A.R.P. denomination. This was meagre knowledge for a minister's son in those years and, besides, although I had been christened in a religious ceremony at my birthplace in Coweta County in west Georgia, I had never had the experience of being baptized. And more than that, purposely or not, I had never been asked or ordered to attend Sunday-school. When I did go to Sunday-school, it was because my playmates attended and I wanted to be with them.

It was not surprising to me, since it was in keeping with the privilege of being permitted to learn about life as I lived it, that it was not my own father, but a Jewish storekeeper in Charlotte, North Carolina, who made me aware that religious faiths other than that of the A.R.P. existed in the world and that it was possible for human compassion to cross existing religious boundaries. The storekeeper's name was Mr. Goldstein and he owned a family clothing and shoe store on Trade Street in the business centre of Charlotte.

I was riding my bicycle along the street in the summer afternoon and looking for tin foil in discarded cigarette packs. I had already salvaged enough tin foil to make a ball about the size of a small cantaloup and hoped to get enough to be paid a quarter for it when I sold it to a junk dealer in an alley behind Tryon Street.

I stopped in front of Mr. Goldstein's clothing and shoe store to pick up a crumpled cigarette pack from the gutter and he came out to the kerb and asked me if I wanted a job delivering shoes for him. It was the first time I had ever been offered a job in the business world and I must have been too surprised to say anything. He put his hand on my shoulder and gripped it as if afraid I would leave and not take the job. Then again he asked me if I would work for him. He said he would pay me two dollars a week for working every afternoon except Saturday and Sunday.

The certainty of earning two dollars a week was much more appealing than the uncertainty of finding enough tin foil on the streets to earn twenty-five cents occasionally and I eagerly agreed to take the job. Mr. Goldstein took me into the store, handed me a box of shoes, and wrote the delivery address on a slip of paper. I pedalled my bicycle for what seemed like several miles and finally got to the address on Statesville Avenue near the city limits.

After delivering the shoes to the customer, I went back downtown, but it was already becoming dark and Mr. Goldstein had locked the door of his store and gone away. I was late for supper when I got home and I fully expected to be scolded and told that I could not keep my job. However, my parents said that since I had agreed to work by the week for Mr. Goldstein, I should keep my part of the agreement, and so I went back to the store the next afternoon promptly at one o'clock.

The following Friday afternoon, the end of my first week working for Mr. Goldstein, and pay-day, I was given two boxes of shoes to deliver at the same address and instructed to collect two dollars for one pair and to bring the other pair back to the store. Mr. Goldstein explained that the shoes were in two sizes for a boy

5]

about twelve years old and that the boy's mother would keep the pair that fitted best.

When I got to the address on South Boulevard where the shoes were to be delivered, I immediately recognized the small, unpainted, weather-greyed house that was in the same neighbourhood where I lived.

It was the home of two of my playmates and I had often gone there to play with them in the back yard. Their mother was a widow and she did sewing and ironing by the day whenever she could find work in the neighbourhood. The three of them lived in the two-room house with little furniture other than two beds, some chairs, and a large oilcloth-covered table in the rear room. The frail, dark-haired woman was a member of the A.R.P. church where my father was the temporary pastor and she attended services almost every Sunday morning. The two boys, however, had not been to Sunday-school for two months or longer.

While the older boy, whose name was Floyd, was in the house trying on the shoes, his brother Pete and I went to the back yard and played with the train and fire engine they kept in a shed they had built with sides of wooden packing-cases and pieces of tin roofing.

In a little while their mother called me to the rear porch and handed me two dollars and one of the boxes of shoes. Then she said that the larger pair fitted Floyd and that I would see him at the picnic the Sunday-school was having in a park the next afternoon. When I asked if Pete would be at the picnic, she said he would have to stay at home because she could buy only one pair of shoes and did not want him to go to the Sunday-school picnic barefooted.

I took the money and the box of shoes and started to get on my bicycle to go back to the store on Trade Street. It was then that I saw Floyd come to the porch wearing

[6

his new pair of shoes, and I looked around at Pete. All I could think of was that Mr. Goldstein would give me two dollars in pay when I got back to the store and that the smaller size of shoes would probably fit Pete because he was a year younger than his brother. I went to the porch and put the box of shoes on the steps and then I got on my bicycle and pedalled up South Boulevard as fast as I could.

When I got back to the store, I gave Mr. Goldstein the two dollars I had collected and then began trying to explain why I had not brought back the other pair of shoes as he had told me to do. Before he could say anything, I told him that I wanted him to keep the two dollars he had agreed to pay me and to use it to pay for the shoes I had left for Pete to wear to the Sunday-school picnic the next afternoon.

Mr. Goldstein sat down on a stool and said nothing for a long time. It was late in the afternoon then, and there were no customers in the store. Presently he looked up and beckoned to me with a motion of his head. When I came closer, he pointed for me to sit down on the counter near him.

First, he asked what church I attended, and then he asked what my father did for a living. After that he looked up at me and shook his head back and forth with a solemn expression on his face.

There was a long silence. Then Mr. Goldstein said he would never be able to understand as long as he lived how Christians and gentiles ever made a living in business and kept from going bankrupt. Turning around and looking up at me, he told me that Jewish people were just as kind-hearted and sentimental and human as Christians, but that Jews had learned long ago to earn money first and then give some of it away later for a

7]

good cause. He said that I ought to keep that in mind if I expected to make a living in business and keep out of bankruptcy courts when I grew up.

It was closing time for the store. Mr. Goldstein got up from the stool, talking aloud to himself, and began turning out the lights. I could not hear anything he was saying, but just before he was ready to lock the front door, he handed me a dollar. As he did that, he said he owed me two dollars for a week's salary and that I owed him two dollars for the shoes I had given away and that the only thing to do about it was for each of us to contribute a dollar for Pete's shoes.

When I went home and told my father what had happened, he said it proved that a man did not have to be a Presbyterian or a Baptist or a Methodist or anything else, in order to be blessed with the goodness of humanity. Then Ira Sylvester said he had needed a new pair of shoes for a long time and that he was going to Mr. Goldstein's store the first thing Monday morning and buy a pair.

I had to give up my job at Mr. Goldstein's store when we moved from Charlotte to Tampa, Florida, at the end of summer. It was in Tampa that I became aware for the first time that some white Southern people refused to share religious services with persons whose colour of skin was darker than their own—and including my dark-skinned, black-haired father.

During those years, Ira Sylvester was secretary of the home mission board of the A.R.P. synod, and he frequently went to one of the churches that was in financial difficulty or where there was so much dissension among members of a congregation that the continued existence of that particular church was threatened. At a time like that, he was charged with the responsibility of attempting to readjust the condition that he considered to be the cause of trouble. There were times when he was successful in his efforts to unite two opposing factions and there were times when he was unable to persuade either side to agree to accept or even to discuss the suggestions he offered.

The Tampa church was in the Spanish-speaking neighbourhood of Ybor City where many Cubans lived and worked in the cigar factories. It was a recently-organized mission that had been established by a group of retired farmers and merchants from Mississippi, Alabama, and Georgia and it had a small congregation of less than fifty members at the time. As a means of making the church self-supporting, it was my father's plan to increase attendance and contributions by inviting Cubans who lived near by to come to Sunday services.

After several weeks, Ira Sylvester said he was convinced that it was a mistake to expect Spanish-speaking Cubans to accept Scotch–Irish Protestantism without some introduction to its dogma. Knowing that all Cubans in Ybor City were not committed to Catholicism, he was sure that some of them would be inclined to attend Protestant church services if sermons were shorter and more music provided.

In order that the Cubans would have a better understanding of the words they were singing, the English-language psalms were translated into Spanish and then, so as to enliven the tempo of the music, the organ was exchanged for a piano. It was not long until more than half of the original membership of retired farmers and merchants had stopped attending services and contributing to the support of the church.

However, as the attendance of the original members decreased, the Cuban attendance increased. It was not long until the small wooden church was almost completely filled every Sunday morning and evening. And contributions had increased to such an extent that there was enough money in the church treasury to replace the leaking rusty roof with shiny new tin roofing.

Just a few weeks before we were planning to leave Florida and move to Virginia, two of the elders told Ira Sylvester they wanted him to resign and leave town immediately. When he asked for an explanation, he was told that the white people who had been born and raised in the tradition of the South were not going to violate their principles by attending church with dark-skinned Cubans who resembled half-breed Negroes, that the church had been built for white people only to worship God, and that they would rather see the church closed or burned to ashes than let it be desecrated by people who were not suitably white. They said it was known all over Tampa and that section of Florida that some of the people who passed for Cubans were actually part-Negro, just as there were admitted Negroes who were part-Cuban, and that Southern white people were not going to associate in the same building with people whose colour of skin was just as dark as that of an ordinary mulatto.

When my father asked if they were dissatisfied with him as a minister in any other way, one of the elders admitted that there was one more thing that they wanted to say. He was told that some of the original members felt uneasy about the darkness of his skin, because he was no lighter in colour than some of the Cubans who came to church services.

Ira Sylvester told the elders that he had no way of verifying the purity of his Anglo-Saxon heritage, because his Scottish ancestors had left Scotland and mingled with the Irish and Huguenots—and probably with American Indians, too—but that he did not think his racial mixture had discoloured his religious convictions.

The two men left without shaking hands or saying good-bye when Ira Sylvester told them that he had come to take charge of the church for six months and would not be leaving before the end of that time.

When I was seventeen years old, I had completed the final year of high school in Wrens, Georgia, and I planned to go away to college in the fall. In the meantime, I had been able to get a summer job as a mason's helper in Calhoun, Georgia, not far from Chattanooga, Tennessee. I had been told that my work would be to mix mortar and carry hods of brick for a church under construction. The pay was to be twenty-five cents an hour from seven-thirty to five-thirty and the cost of room and board would be a dollar a day.

By that time, having been with my parents in numerous places in all the states of the South and having lived the life of a minister's son during those years, I had accumulated a considerable amount of religious experience and I felt confident of being able to adjust to life wherever I went. Consequently, I did not expect to be in need of religious advice when I was to live away from home for the first time and I would have been surprised if my father had even mentioned about religion when I was leaving home for the summer job in north Georgia. He knew that my knowledge of the religious side of life was no longer confined to what I had observed in A.R.P. churches.

By that time there had been many memorable occasions

11]

in the Southern states from Virginia to Florida to Arkansas when I had been with I.S. in churches of various faiths and denominations. We had gone to Church of God all-night camp-meetings, Holy Roller exhibitions on splintery wooden floors, Primitive Christian baptismal immersions in muddy creeks, Seventh Day Adventist foot-washings, Body of Christ blood-drinking communions, Kingdom of God snake-handlings, Full Redeemer glossolalia* services, Fire Baptized Holiness street-corner rallies, Catholic mass at midnight on Christmas Eve, the rituals of Jewish synagogues, and to philosophical lectures in Unitarian churches.

After attending a calm and dignified religious service performed with a series of songs and prayers, usually there would be favourable comments by I.S. about the architecture of the church or the quality of the choir music. But I.S. rarely had anything to say after taking me to listen to a prolonged and unintelligible babble in the Unknown Tongue, or to see people rolling in the throes of ecstasy on a church floor, or to watch a Sanctified preacher hit his head with an axe handle until he had achieved a state of semi-conscious delirium. However, it is probable that his motive, aside from his own avid interest in the subject, was to provide an educational field course for me in all contemporary religious practices.

Also at this time, after having been in the shadow of the steeple during all those early years, it was unexpected to hear I.S. say that I should know enough about life by then to decide for myself if I ever wished to attend a religious service again or to become a member of a church of any denomination.

* Glossolalia: an unintelligible litany loudly spoken by members of a congregation uttering individual prayers and not speaking in unison. It is also known as speaking in the Unknown Tongue.

[12

Having been offered this freedom of choice, I wondered if I would ever lose interest in observing the spectacle of religious practices as I grew older. I thought not. I had been so close to evangelical religion for so many years that I had the feeling that even if I remained unchurched I would want to continue watching the effect its emotional appeal had on people as time went on.

Now, after forty-odd years, it would seem reasonable to expect that, in contrast, a recollection of the white Anglo-Saxon Protestant religious practices of the historical 'twenties and an observation of those of the contemporary 'sixties would serve to illuminate to some degree the churchly life of the two eras of the Deep South.

Two

WHILE GROWING UP in the South during those early years of the century, and before going away from home for the first time, what was always of interest to me was hearing I.S. tell about some experience he had had while on one of his frequent trips preaching or investigating a dispute or disruption in one of the A.R.P. churches. Sometimes it was as if I were listening to a detective or secret agent talk about an adventure in a far-away place even if all that had happened was that somebody had stolen his suitcase in a railroad station.

There were times when I.S. would be away from home for as long as a week or more, always travelling on trains when the time was too short or the distance too long for automobile trips on unpaved roads. He would come back to where we happened to be living at the time with an exciting tale about having been to places with such unusual names as Live Oak, Florida, and Red Level, Alabama, and Why Not, Mississippi.

When he came home from a long train trip, his clothing always had the tingling smell of the coal smoke of steam engines. Since he usually brought me the timetable of the railroad on which he had been travelling, it was not long until I felt sure that I could become proficient in being able to identify the particular railroad on which he had travelled merely by the odour of the coal smoke that saturated his clothing.

Some railroads used bituminous coal that had been mined in Virginia and West Virginia, while other railroads fired their steam engines with coal from Kentucky, Tennessee, and Alabama. I wanted to be able to detect the difference in odour, just as I had seen the hue of engine smoke—dark brown to dark grey to coal black—that varied from one railroad to another. If it happened to be summer and I.S. had not worn his coat on the train, it was still easy enough to detect a particular odour by shaking the cinders from his hatband and rubbing them vigorously between the palms of my hands.

As time went on, the distinctive smell of coal smoke of the Southern, Seaboard, Atlantic Coast Line, Louisville and Nashville, and other large railroads became easy to detect. However, I was never able to be positive when it came to trying to identify the smaller railroads, such as the Charleston and Western Carolina, the Atlanta and West Point, and the Columbia, Newberry and Laurens, by the smell of the smoke or cinders of their steam engines.

Ira Sylvester was always in good spirits, and usually had several new jokes to tell when he came home from a successful trip. After an unsuccessful trip, though, he was often morose and despondent. It was when he was thoroughly disheartened that he sometimes said there were some people in the world who should never be permitted to join a church of any denomination, and they and everybody else would be better off if they gave up the pretence of practising religion and became the atheists or agnostics they were more suited to be.

Several times when he came home from a particularly unsuccessful trip, I heard Ira Sylvester announce that if he could have his way, he would dissolve the entire congregation of a certain church and sell the land and building to the highest bidder even if the Holy Rollers got possession of the property. Whenever he became deeply discouraged and expressed disdain for uncooperative factions in a congregation, he would say that such people would have a better chance of going to heaven, if that was what they expected to do, by resigning from the A.R.P. church. The ideal place for them to engage in the practice of their kind of religion was on the floor with the Holy Rollers or in a Sanctified church where they could hit themselves on the head with a mallet or axe handle until they were completely befuddled and woozy.

One of the most memorable of all of Ira Sylvester's unsuccessful trips was the time he came home and vowed that he would resign if ever again he had to contend with a similar aggravating group of professed Christians. This was after he had travelled on three different railroads and I had been unable, because of the mingled odour of engine smoke, to identify a single one of them. I was just as unhappy about this failure of mine as he was about the results of his trip.

In this particular instance, as he told about the church he had visited, approximately half of the members wanted to carpet the floor of the church and all the others opposed the idea. He said when he got to the town where the church was located, he found that every member had taken a firm and apparently an unalterable stand on one side or the other and that he could find no neutral or reasonable person in the whole congregation to help in trying to reach a satisfactory solution. Even the pastor declined to help. The pastor had been threatened by both factions and told that his salary would be stopped if he favoured one faction over the other.

As a result of the controversy, the bare-floor and the carpet-floor advocates had stopped speaking to one another, two divorces had occurred in intermarried families, and there had been a shooting affray in which one member was killed and another paralysed for life.

And that was not all. The electric power company was threatening to turn off the lights because the bill had not been paid; the fire insurance premium on the church building was three months past due and a final notice had been sent stating that the policy would be cancelled unless payment was received within ten days; and the Negro sexton said he was not going to ring the church bell or sweep the floor or wash the windows until something was done about his pay for the past four months.

The deacons continued to pass the collection plates every Sunday, but neither the bare-floor nor the carpet-floor advocates would contribute. Both factions had been adamant and uncompromising for nearly six months and all members continued to say they would not contribute a penny for the support of the church unless they could have their way.

The conflict within the congregation of approximately two hundred persons began the previous year when some members complained that many of the others were disrupting and profaning the sacredness of religious services and the worship of God by loudly thumping the heels of their shoes on the bare floor and keeping time with the music during both choir and congregational singing.

The floor-thumping members contended that all good Christians should keep time to church music by thumping

[18

their feet and that a bare wooden floor was necessary so that the thumping would be loud and distinct.

When I.S. came home after being away almost a week that time, he said he had told the members that the best suggestion he could offer under the circumstances was for them to eliminate all choir and congregational singing for a trial period of two or three months, and to devote the entire church hour to listening to the pastor's sermon.

When the suggestion was rejected by both factions, he told them that as long as they were obviously unwilling to be reasonable, and gave no indication of a desire to find a way to settle the controversy, he would have to go away and wait for everybody concerned to have a change of mind.

After such an unsuccessful effort to unite the two quarrelling factions in that particular church, I.S. was glum and discouraged and he talked about resigning as secretary of the home mission board. He was convinced that the cause of trouble and dissension in that church, as in many others, was due to the fact that many members became so pre-occupied with the rituals and manifestations of religion that they were unable to appreciate the purpose of religion itself. He said he was not the kind of person who had the patience to deal with such unreasonable and unrealistic people.

But, as usual, I.S. did not resign as secretary of the home mission board, nor, as he sometimes threatened to do when he was extremely depressed, did he resign from the A.R.P. ministry.

When he did talk about resigning, he would say that he was coming to the conclusion that he had done all he could for the good of the church. He never said what he would do if he resigned from the ministry, but he often remarked that the South was more in need of trained and

19]

professional social welfare workers and public-school teachers than it was of additional ministers and evangelists. At a time like that, he reckoned half the members of any congregation he had ever known were already adequately sold on heaven and the other half were unalterably committed to hell.

As to the controversy between the bare-floor and the carpet-floor advocates, I.S. said that in his opinion it was obviously a hopelessly deadlocked situation with both sides determined not to agree to the slightest compromise and that there was little possibility of the conflict being resolved before the church became completely disorganized. What he had in mind, if the decision were left to him, was to recommend that the church be closed and the property sold to pay outstanding obligations. And as for the members themselves, they could either build two separate churches, one carpeted and one bare-floored, or they could join churches of other denominations that conducted services to their liking.

Finally, I.S. remarked that the bare-floor advocates had made a mistake in the beginning by not becoming members of a traditional foot-thumping and hand-clapping sect, such as the Assembly of God or the Full Faith Gospel, because the psalm-singing A.R.P. organization had never been acclaimed for its appreciation of musical rhythm.

The next time Ira Sylvester went away to investigate and try to find a remedy for a troublesome situation in one of the churches, he returned home a few days later well pleased with what he had been able to accomplish. It was winter and he was wearing a dark grey overcoat that was thoroughly saturated with the pungent sweet smell of what I was sure was Atlantic Coast Line engine smoke. When he took the timetable from his pocket, it was good to know that once more I had been able to identify the sulphurous coal-smoke odour with a particular railroad.

All Ira Sylvester had known about the situation before leaving home to investigate was that the particular church had a membership of more than three hundred persons; that it was a wealthy congregation and the church had never before been in financial difficulty; that the pastor was a young man recently graduated from a theological seminary and had not had any previous pastoral experience; and, most important of all, that somebody had been stealing a considerable amount of money during a period of several months from the Sunday morning collection.

Among the first things he found out when he began asking questions was that the money deposited in the church's bank account on Monday mornings had dwindled to less than half of normal. As a consequence, some bills had gone unpaid and the pastor was receiving much less than his agreed-upon salary.

Ira Sylvester said that none of the elders actually accused any of the four deacons of taking money that was contributed at the Sunday services, but that some of them intimated that they suspected a recently appointed deacon of helping himself to more than half of the contributions.

The new deacon had many relatives in the congregation and he was a young bachelor who had recently opened an insurance agency. Even though his insurance business appeared to be profitable, it was well known in town that his office rent was not being paid on time and nor was his secretary's salary.

It was an unusual situation, because in most churches

there was no opportunity for a newly appointed deacon to take money from the Sunday collections. Besides, deacons were considered to be men of unquestioned honesty who would never be tempted to steal. However, it had been the policy of this particular church for many years to impress upon the most recently appointed deacon the fact that he had been given a position of responsibility by entrusting him with the church's money overnight until it could be deposited in the bank on Monday morning.

Those who had become suspicious of the new deacon were afraid that if he were falsely accused, and afterwards found to be innocent, either his numerous relatives would leave the church and join another denomination or, if they did remain as members, there would be damaging dissension in the congregation for many years to come.

It had been proposed by an elder that one of the other deacons take the money home overnight, but it was decided that would be the same as making a direct accusation, just as it would be if a safe were installed in the church for the same purpose.

Then for a while it had been suspected that a bank clerk might be the person to be charged with the theft, but an investigation by the directors of the bank disclosed no such embezzlement.

What the elders wanted to avoid above all was a public scandal in the church, and for that reason they were opposed to hiring a detective or investigator which might lead to the deacon's arrest by the police for stealing. They said such things had been known in churches of some of the other denominations, but it was unthinkable that an A.R.P. church would ever be subjected to such indignity.

As it happened, I.S. spent a day talking to each of the elders and another day talking to various members of the church, none of whom was willing to confront the suspected deacon, and then he spent an evening with the young pastor.

The pastor, a nervous man with thinning sandy-coloured hair and still unmarried, was fearful that a public disclosure of the guilty person would be damaging to his career as a minister. He begged I.S. to leave town immediately without investigating further at that time and then to come back after a few months if necessary. It was his ambition to become pastor of a church in another state that had a much larger and more wealthy congregation and where he would receive a salary twice as big as he could ever expect in his present position.

The young minister did not hesitate to admit that he was less concerned about money being taken from the contributions than he was about the possibility of the elders of the other church hearing about the matter. If the suspected deacon were charged with theft and admitted his guilt, it would reflect on him as a minister and harm his reputation so badly that the offer he expected to receive within a few weeks would surely be withdrawn.

Then he told I.S. that an additional reason for his wanting to keep the matter quiet was because he was engaged to marry the daughter of a wealthy member of the church to which he hoped to be called as pastor and he might lose that opportunity to benefit himself, too.

At the end of the evening when I.S. was leaving to walk back to the hotel, he told the young minister that he had come there to help the entire congregation in a serious matter, not to help him obtain a higher salary elsewhere and marry into a wealthy family.

I.S. said the only other thing he should have mentioned at the time was that it was unfortunate a young man with such an attitude should have entered the ministry and

23]

that he ought to leave it and find some other occupation as soon as possible.

The next morning he went to the insurance office to talk to the young deacon. They talked about many things for an hour or longer, not once mentioning the church's missing money, and long before the end of that time he was certain he had discovered why the money was being taken from the Sunday morning collections.

All he had to do after that, my father said, was to ask the young man what luck he was having with the bets he was placing on horse races. When he admitted that the losses were more than he could afford and, besides, that his insurance agency was not making expenses, I.S. suggested he spend six full days a week working at the insurance business and devote all of Sunday, by not attending church services, to the study of racing forms and charts.

I.S. said there was no need to suggest that the young deacon resign, since it was easy to tell by the expression of gratitude and relief on the young man's face that he realized how fortunate he was not to be publicly charged with taking church money to make bets on horse races. Both of them knew that he had helped himself to church money for the last time and that in the future, if he attended services after resigning as deacon, he would sit in a rear pew and put money into the collection plate instead of taking from it.

Three

AS IT HAS BEEN now for several generations, and with more generations to come, the Cumberland range of mountains in Kentucky and Tennessee is an insular region of southern Appalachia where each year money becomes more scarce and religion becomes increasingly plentiful.

Agriculture was never a sustaining occupation in a land of mountainous slopes and rocky ravines for the Anglo-Saxon settlers and their descendants. For a time, coal-mining provided jobs, and then mechanized strip-mining of coal inevitably reduced employment as each year went by. But evangelistic and fundamentalistic religion has thrived and flourished in the mother country of the Cumberlands for the past half-century as nowhere else in the United States.

While hunger and poverty and despair increased from year to year, religious ecstasy became the only available narcotic to dull the pain of living. Hope of heaven was all there was to live for on earth and all it took to enliven hope was a frequent priming of emotional glands with promises of a better life after death. Evangelism has always promised more for the future than any government can provide for the present.

A scarcity of money beginning early in the present century, which was the result of the lack of opportunity for many persons of the Cumberlands to earn an adequate living in agriculture and mining, instituted the custom of bartering and swapping among neighbours and strangers as a means of survival and livelihood.

It was inevitable in a region where it was an economic necessity to resort to primitive barter and swap that a plenitude of hell-fire-and-brimstone and pearly-gates-of-heaven evangelistic Protestantism would make hard-core religion a product eagerly sought by the impoverished and unenlightened Southerners of Anglo-Saxon descent who had become imprisoned there.

Bartering and swapping in the Cumberlands, now as in the past, takes place close to home while ecstatic, emotional, prolific, Cumberland-style evangelistic religion is in such ample supply that each year a surplus is exported with missionary zeal. The greater part of the surplus goes to other Southern states, from Virginia and the Carolinas to Arkansas and Louisiana. And even after all that there is still enough missionary zeal remaining to evangelize portions of the Midwest, from Ohio to Missouri, and the Southwest, from Texas to California.

This mountain-locked hinterland of eastern Kentucky and eastern Tennessee, a sprawling settlement wo hundred years old with a population of several hundred thousand, is the native ground of the white Anglo-Saxon Protestant—the WASP—and the breeding place of innumerable evangelistic and fundamentalistic sects and faiths—including separatists, divisionists, revisionists, conformists, and non-conformists—ranging from Holy Rollers and Snake-Handlers to Foot-Washers and Hard Shell Baptists.

The precept of fundamentalism is the guiding spirit of all Cumberland-style religions and this leads inevitably to reactionary and ultra-conservative principles and conduct in secular life.

A Cumberland religious zealot, whether an ordained minister, an unordained evangelist, or a lay-brother, is a prime prospect for membership, and often for leadership, in segregationist and similar extremist organizations when he goes into the outside world. After a generation or so, his descendants are likely to be among the sheet-wearing members of a poor man's militantly reactionary club, such as the Ku-Klux-Klan, or to be dues-paying supporters of a rich man's defiantly ultra-conservative club, such as the Citizens' Council.

In such an environment of unyielding traditions and steadfast fundamentalism, it is to be expected that the social and political changes that have been commonplace elsewhere in the United States in recent years should be resisted in the Cumberlands. As a consequence, few noticeable changes have taken place there between the early 'twenties and the late 'sixties.

Apart from the inevitable alterations in the style of clothing, the only immediately recognizable change has been the transformation of wagons into trucks and hitching posts into parking meters. Otherwise, life among the lean-limbed and sharply-profiled descendants of the Scotch-Irish and English settlers of the eighteenth and twentieth centuries is relatively unchanged and unchanging.

The first time I was ever in the Cumberlands was shortly before the First World War. I was travelling with my father on one of his frequent trips somewhere in the South, although this time he was on personal business

27]

and not on a mission for the A.R.P. synod. Ira Sylvester had said he wanted me to go with him to the Cumberlands so I could see for myself while I was still young how people lived in that part of the world.

It was summer and the dirt roads were dry and dusty. We had come in a Ford touring car with the top down all the way from west Tennessee to eastern Kentucky to place an order for a special kind of custom-made buggy.

For one thing, Ira Sylvester wanted a wide-track buggy instead of the standard style, and then it was his belief that the best hickory, oak, and walnut for wheels, shafts, and body grew in the Cumberlands and we had the name and address of a buggy-maker who had agreed by letter to follow exact specifications. The buggy was a necessity as a means of transportation in winter in west Tennessee when the unpaved country roads in those days were too slippery and miry for automobile travel.

We stopped early one afternoon in a town in the Cumberlands and got a room for the night in the hotel. It was too early then for supper and we walked down the main street to see the town. After walking several blocks, we came to a group of six or eight men who were seated on benches and wooden boxes in front of a hardware and harness store. One of the men raised his hand in greeting and invited us to sit down and rest a while.

The man sitting next to Ira Sylvester said he was a farmer and lived on a small patch of land up one of the creeks and raised a little corn and tobacco and kept a few hogs. In addition to that, he had a small coal-hole behind his house and worked it enough to get coal for cooking and heating. He said that he made a fair living for his family by bartering what he could spare for what he needed in the stores and rarely saw any real money.

Ira Sylvester told the Kentuckian that he was a

Presbyterian minister from west Tennessee and that we had come all that distance to have a buggy made of genuine Cumberland wood.

They talked for a while about the best kind of spoke wood and shaft wood for a buggy, and then the farmer reached into his overall pocket and offered to swap knives with my father. They compared blades and bone-handles and trademarks of each other's pocket-knives for a long time while each one waited for the other to make the first offer.

Finally, the offer was made by the farmer to swap for fifty cents to boot. Ira Sylvester offered to give him twenty-five cents to boot. In the end, they swapped for thirty cents.

The man who had gained thirty cents on the trade put the money into his pocket and patted it appreciatively. After that, he said, he was in good shape to go to church the next Sunday and not be blessed-out by the preacher again as he had been the previous Sunday, when he did not even have a five-cent piece to put into the collection basket.

When we got up to leave and go back to the hotel to eat supper, he shook hands with Ira Sylvester and said he hoped there would be no hard feelings for having taken swap-money from a Presbyterian preacher to give to a Pentecostal preacher.

Ira Sylvester told him not to worry because the money would be used for a good religious purpose. The man shook his head and said it might be true with the Presbyterians, but the Pentecostal preacher always grabbed the money from the collection basket and put it straight into his pants' pocket before God had a chance to see how much it was.

·　　·　　·　　·　　·

In the coal region of the Cumberlands in the latter part of the 'sixties, along the tragic valley of poverty and degradation from Middlesboro to Pineville to Harlan, there may be even less to barter and swap than there was nearly a half-century ago. Along the trains and footpaths in the ravines, out of sight of paved roads and highways, shacks and cabins tilt and sag and rot on the verge of collapse in the shadow of the green summer thatch of white oaks and black walnuts. The faces of the young people are blank with despair and the voices of the old people are saying that all is lost and tomorrow will be like yesterday and today—unless it is worse.

A government plan to alleviate poverty is remote and unseen and faintly rumoured, but close at hand there is inspirational religion in a church for immediate comfort and the traditional ceremony of swapping knives and watches for companionship and conversation—and hopefully for profit.

As a lean-faced Cumberland mountaineer said, the thing to do while waiting to take the trip to heaven to live in comfort with Jesus is to try to make the best possible swaps on earth and bring in a quarter or a half-dollar now and then.

Only last Sunday morning when I fixed up and went to preaching up the creek, I didn't have a thin dime to my name to put in the collection box when the deacons started making their rounds.

One of them deacons—that old Ed Hawkins—kept on shoving the box right at me against my breast-bone like he thought I was asleep and had to be woke up. He knowed I wasn't sleeping but he wouldn't let on about it. He just kept on pestering me so much I had to lift up and shove the box right back at him with my elbow, like this. That wasn't the first time I'd been in that fix in church with no money at all, but everybody was looking and

[30

staring at me and I felt like sticking my tail between my hind legs if I'd been some old dog. Deacons sure can make you feel bad about being poor like me. And that old Ed Hawkins is the worst of all.

I always go to church on Sundays to get my soul saved once a week like the preacher says I'd better—and every time when there's a revival meeting, too—and the last time which was last Sunday I was scared clean through to my deep bones I wasn't going to get it saved to last out the week.

The preacher knowed I'd had a quarter in cash money only two days before that on Friday and I could see him standing up there at the pulpit looking straight down at me all the time I wasn't putting that quarter in the collection box. What he didn't know was that it'd already been spent.

The way how the preacher come to know I had that quarter to begin with, which was before I spent it paying for a can of snuff right here at the store, was because me and him swapped pocket-knives that Friday before and he'd handed over to me that quarter to boot and told me to be sure to put the quarter in the collection box on Sunday if I expected him to save my soul for me so I could go to heaven and live up there with Jesus.

I'd told the preacher with the honest truth I'd sure drop it in the box on Sunday. But then when after he'd got up and walked off, I started wanting snuff pretty bad and that's when I couldn't hold back and went in the store and spent it for a can. That made me out a big liar, but I just couldn't help myself. Everybody knows how it is when you get a belly-gripping craving for a little snuff.

Anyhow, I knowed what was coming that last Sunday morning, all right. I sure did. The preacher got up and started in preaching hard and heavy right after the deacons finished taking up the collection and he preached right straight at me all the time like nobody else but me was in the whole church. There was maybe another forty or so people in the pews, but that didn't make no

31]

difference to him. I tell you, he was real mad. And all because he didn't get his quarter back after a fair-and-square swap. He didn't come right out and call me by name, but he came close to doing it. He was saying all he could about how Jesus was going to slam the gates shut and lock up and keep big liars out of heaven and send them straight down to hell.

The preacher went on like that for the whole time he was preaching for about a whole hour and had me squirming around all the time and I thought he wasn't never going to let up on me.

When he got through, though, he ended up saying Jesus might forgive folks for telling lies if they was sorry what they'd lied about and made up for it double the next time they had the chance. I knowed exactly what he meant by that. He meant if I doubled up the quarter and put in a half-dollar in the collection box next Sunday I'd be all right and get my soul saved so I could go to heaven and live easy with all the other good people in the world.

And so, well, I'm a half-dollar to the good now from swapping knives with that fellow who was here from Pineville a little while ago and that's what I'm so pleased about now. I've got the one quarter I didn't put in last Sunday and the other quarter for next Sunday to double up with. That'll make me even. I can look the preacher straight in the face when I'm sitting there in the pew and he won't have nothing against me to blame me for and call me a liar this time. He won't have no excuse for not saving my soul for one more week, anyhow.

I've been mighty particular about keeping on the good side of preachers all my life and I'm going to keep on staying on that side, too. This here preacher who's preaching here now is a hard man about religion, I tell you, and he won't skip a chance to say you're going to lose your soul to the devil and end up in hell instead of heaven if you don't do all the time like he says. He ain't like some of the easy-going preachers I've heard preach in the past who act like they're scared to talk out real loud. This one keeps me scared half to death.

[32

This preacher I've been talking about is a Sanctified preacher. I tell you, he's a hard man about religion and don't think he won't bear down on you. He can shout good and loud and I'm satisfied that's the best kind. I've been going to some church or another all my life, but I've switched over to the true religion now and joined up with the Sanctifieds. I done that just because of him. I wouldn't go back to easy-going and soft-talking religion for nothing in the world now.

He's the same preacher who took my oldest boy to one side one Sunday after preaching and told him he wanted him to be a preacher. I don't know all of what he said to the boy, but some of it must've scared the daylights out of him, because one thing he said was he was going to quit praying for the boy's soul and he'd end up with the devil in hell instead of in heaven with Jesus if he didn't drop everything and start in preaching.

The boy was nearly past being thirty years old then and was trying to get by doing a little farming on a piece of ground about a mile up the creek from here. He'd been married a good eight years and already had five young ones and another one coming to his wife. The preacher said having a family like that didn't make a bit of difference and that he'd better get started preaching right away if he didn't want to lose his soul and end up in hell.

It wasn't no fault of his own, but the boy hadn't been to school more than three or four years in his whole life and never was none too smart in general. But he could make out some of what was in the Bible and the preacher said that was good enough. He showed the boy how to act when he prayed in the pulpit and told him some things to pray about and then sent him and his whole family down in Tennessee in the back of a truck where the Sanctifieds aimed to set up a new church and needed a preacher right away to get going. He said the best preachers in the whole world got born and raised right around here in these mountains and that was why he'd picked out my boy to be one and go down in Tennessee and get a new church

33]

started for some people down there who wanted to get the true religion real bad.

That was about two years ago when that happened and me and my wife don't know nothing about how the boy and his wife and family is making out down there. But the preacher says he prays for the boy once a week for sure and don't worry none about it because God's taking care of him, anyhow.

I'm real proud of my oldest boy being a Sanctified preacher down there somewhere in Tennessee and that's why I try my best to make some good swaps every chance I get so I'll have a quarter for the collection box for this here preacher every Sunday when the deacons pass it to me.

That don't mean I don't try to make some more other trades and get the benefit, too. I'm always needing fifty cents or a dollar to buy something I need in the store I can't swap for that takes cash money the storekeeper wants for it. That's why I like to see strangers stop by. Strangers always have more cash money on them than home folks.

The rest of the time I can manage somehow to get along pretty well. I barter now and then with some potatoes or a sack of corn meal and maybe some fresh hog meat when a neighbour wants to make a trade like that. My wife's mighty good making hog-liver mush and that's nearly always good for some barter, too.

I used to have a little still but I don't no more. I quit making mash when I joined up with the Sanctifieds. The preacher said he didn't want none of his members getting caught and sent off to jail and couldn't come to church no more. If I want a drink now and then, I get it with a swap of something.

And day in and day out I'm a good religious church member of the Sanctifieds and never have to worry about which way my soul's going when I have a little money for the preacher's collection box. I tell you, it sure is a good feeling deep down inside to know you've got a boy out in the world preaching and saving other folks' souls

[34

while I'm right here not worrying none at all about my own soul and knowing I'm going to heaven to be with Jesus when I die.

I'll bet you there's a lot of sinful people all over the world wishing right now they could be like me. When you know you're never going to have much of nothing in this life down here, anyhow, the smart thing to do is quit being a liar or some other kind of sinner.

It's a big comfort knowing you've got a fine bounty waiting for you when you get to heaven and not have to worry none about running the risk of maybe getting cheated like it is down here every time you swap knives or watches with a stranger you never saw or heard tell of before. I tell you, it's a risky thing living down here on this earth.

Four

IN THE REMOTENESS of the Cumberlands, the study of
theology as preparation for entering the ministry as an
occupation or profession has not often been a prerequisite
for Protestant Scotch–Irish and other Anglo-Saxons who
receive the call to preach.

Even though it might be realized that adequate education and training is a necessary requirement in order
to qualify as teachers in public schools, preaching and
praying comes to the Cumberland native with such
ease that the study of theology is usually considered to
be a waste of time. When you already know by experience how to hammer a nail or pluck a chicken, there
is no sense in going through the motions of pretending to take instruction in what you already know to
perfection.

Nevertheless, there is no other region in America
comparable in area where such a large number of people
of both sexes, professing and adhering to the strict
and uncompromising precepts of old-time Protestant
fundamentalism, are destined to become preachers and
evangelists, ordained or unordained, at some age between fifteen and sixty. It is possible that Bible-carrying
evangelists even outnumber the guitar-carrying folk-
singers going down the valley roads of the Cumberlands

37]

to Nashville to seek fame and fortune in Grand Old Opery.*

Educated in theology or not, a person who is convinced that he has received the divine call to preach has a decision to make before he can begin his evangelistic career either at home or in some other Southern state. This is because, even though all Cumberland-style religion derives from the Bible, some sects use only the Old Testament as inspiration for the worship of God while other sects use only the New Testament to glorify Jesus Christ.

If the prospective preacher or evangelist has not been previously indoctrinated, however, he can avoid having to make a decision between God and Jesus Christ by joining a sect that uses the whole Bible for its religious dogma.

Generally conservative and frequently reactionary, whether evangelistic, fundamentalistic, or dedicated lay-members, these men and women of the Cumberlands who have received the call are single-minded in religion, politics, and social life. They cling to their religious heritage and the community customs that originated from generations in the past.

Like their forefathers—dissident Baptists, Methodists, and Presbyterians who organized new sects to their liking when the mother churches ceased to be fundamentalistic and became ritualistic—they do not hesitate to leave an established church when they are displeased with modernized services. This is when another new sect is formed and dedicated to extreme fundamentalism.

* Grand Old Opery: a concert of folk-songs and hill-billy or country music using electrically-amplified guitars. Nashville, Tennessee, claims the distinction of originating and perpetuating Grand Old Opery.

In this competitive religious environment, a man or woman who has entertained a vision in the night or who otherwise has become imbued with the emotional urge and the religious fervour to become a minister or evangelist is not going to waste much time making up his mind about the kind of religion he is going to preach. Any kind of religion will do, but the rousing showmanship of evangelism produces better and quicker results, in terms of money and emotional response, than sedate and dignified worship.

When an evangelistic service reaches its climax, the alternating quavers of fear and elation have an immediate reaction upon the susceptible mind of an emotionally aroused mountaineer or low-lander. And when any such person, citified or countrified, has been convinced that he needs soul-saving religion, he wants it here and now without delay and he will readily contribute what money he can afford to pay for it.

The major source of elemental evangelism—like its lively adjunct, the mountain music and lyrical lament of folk-songs—continues after nearly two hundred years to be those portions of Virginia, Kentucky, and Tennessee in the Cumberland and Blue Ridge Mountains of Appalachia.

While the effervescent source in this mountain region continues after all this time to be constant and undiminished, its evangelism loses some of its primitivism and tends to become less exuberant and more sophisticated when it gravitates southward from the mountains to the Piedmont of the Carolinas, Georgia, Alabama, and Mississippi. After the Piedmont, however, when it reaches the red clay hills and sandy coastal plains of the Deep South, its old-time religious flavour is revitalized and its true essence spreads over the countryside and seeps into the cities.

In the industrialized Piedmont, unlike elsewhere in the Deep South, rural camp-meetings have been replaced by suburban brick-walled auditoriums and revival tents by rainproof sheds. Only in the less affluent neighbourhoods are creeks and ponds still used for the rites of total immersion. Elsewhere in the Piedmont, baptismal tanks have been installed in churches, dressing-rooms provided for the baptistery, and the immersion water heated to a comfortable swimming-pool temperature.

However, genuine American evangelism itself has no geographical limitations. It is as effective in one place as another when a crowd gathers and the saving of souls for Jesus Christ is enumerated. And it is at its best when an expert evangelist drips sweat and his voice is trained for the emotional quavers of sincerity.

The frenzied shouting and uninhibited physical gyrations of Brother Smith, an unordained preacher who had a two-week training course in practical evangelism at the Clear Creek Theological School in Kentucky, is as productive of soul-saving results as the studied and personable technique of Billy Graham. And down in the sand-clay country of the Deep South, the evangelistic fifteen-year-old brother and sister twins with amplified guitar, and the Unknown Tongue husband-and-wife team with accordion and tambourine, are just as effective in winning converts as Brother Smith and Billy Graham are with black suits and white neckties and spellbinding oratory.

While numerically the evangelistic results will likely

[40

be similar in all regions, financially they will differ unless the twins and the married team try harder and preach more often in order to collect contributions comparable to those received at the revivals and crusades conducted by Brother Smith and Billy Graham.

Like the coming of the circus, revival meetings conducted by evangelists with well-known reputations attract large crowds in cities once or twice a year. In smaller places, the church has services every week of the year and could not exist if it did not have the support of members consistently attending services twice on Sunday and often on Wednesday and Saturday nights. It is here, usually in the low-rent residential districts of towns or in impoverished rural areas, that evangelical religion thrives best. This is where one can find a shirt-sleeved, back-slapping, home-folksy meeting place with an atmosphere of informal sociability and entertainment where at the same time sin can be shed and souls saved.

If the time comes, however, when the congregation becomes too large for compatibility and personal friendship, if the minister becomes impersonal, or if the services become too formalized, some of the dissatisfied members are likely to form a splinter group and organize another church that will be to their liking.

Should dissident members make such a move, and leave a church called Full Gospel, they would be likely to name their new church True Full Gospel, Spiritual Full Gospel, or something similar in order that it would have a definite identity of its own. After being established, it would probably be only vaguely affiliated, if at all, with any denomination, synod, conference, or organization.

By remaining independent, a newly established church would not be required to contribute money from church collections to help support schools, orphanages, hospitals, and administrative headquarters in faraway places. Instead, perhaps within a few years, enough money would accumulate to enable the congregation to replace their small, unpainted, wooden structure with a larger, steepled, brick-walled, evangelical temple.

As often happens when an imposing new temple has been built, there is a good possibility that enough additional money will be collected to erect a large electric sign on the roof of the building. The lettering of such a sign, lighted seven nights a week the year around, is usually the same as that on similar evangelical churches: JESUS SAVES.

In a new church, just as in an old church, once a member becomes accustomed to the excitement of a particular type of evangelical religion, he is likely to become unhappy and dissatisfied if his church begins emulating the rituals and formality of the uptown First Baptist church and the high-rent-district Memorial Methodist church. He wants no part of a church that he suspects is dangerously close to instituting the formalized and impersonal rites he associates with the Catholics and Episcopalians.

What an evangelized new convert or an old-time member yearns for at a Sunday service in a fundamentalistic church are lengthy and sorrowful prayers by a voluble Brother or Elder, the minister's inspiring forewarnings of the inevitability of death, the stimulating sounds of an electrically-amplified guitar, the humorous remarks of a visiting lady evangelist, the call from the pulpit for him to walk down the aisle and raise his arms in supplication and then to be able once more to renounce sin

[42

in public and declare his unfailing allegiance to Jesus Christ.

The lean-faced, dark-haired, thirty-year-old evangelist had been a part-time coal-miner in the Cumberlands before he came to the Piedmont factory town in North Carolina and was able to get part-time work in a lumber yard. He was married and had three children.

He recalled that before leaving Kentucky and coming to North Carolina he had received a vision soon after being converted and confessing his sins in front of all the people at a revival meeting. God told him in the vision to drop everything and go to North Carolina and save souls for Jesus Christ.

It had taken him almost two months to get to North Carolina after receiving the vision and the reason for the delay was that it had not been easy to find cash buyers for his household goods and hand-tools. He needed cash to buy a second-hand automobile for the long trip since nobody would sell him one on credit.

He said that for several years he had been hearing rumours about wages being much higher in North Carolina towns where there were cigarette factories and textile mills and furniture plants, but that such rumours had nothing to do with his leaving the Cumberlands. He said the only reason for his leaving home and moving to North Carolina was because God had appeared before him in the vision and had ordered him to do so.

Before I stood up in the revival meeting that time and confessed my sins so everybody could hear, I was just about as big a sinner as the worst sinners anybody ever heard about. I lied and fornicated and stole a little something here and there and done all the other sinful things big sinners do.

I didn't belong to no church at all before then, and that's when I'd slip out of the house from my wife and make out like I was going somewhere at night to listen to the preaching in a church. The reason I went off to a church like that was because it was the only place around where there'd be a big crowd of people after dark and you knowed there'd be some girls and women coming and going to their outhouse behind the church.

What I'd make a habit of doing was go around to the back of the church in the dark and find somebody to fornicate with somehow. After that I'd go off in the woods where I knowed I could get hold of some moonshine to drink. I didn't think nothing of stealing some of the makings at somebody's still, neither. There was always plenty of it around and all I had to do was tramp around some in the brush till I stepped on one of the jugs that was covered over with leaves and trash and then take all I wanted of it. If I didn't drink too much of it and lay down too long, I might go back to behind the church and see if I could find somebody willing to let me fornicate some more. That happened nearly every Sunday night when the weather was fine and not too cold or rainy. But one night it started raining when I was out back waiting around like that and there wasn't nothing I could do but go inside the church to keep dry. That's how I came to get converted and ended up seeing the vision.

I tell you, I was just about the biggest sinner than anybody else was around up there where I used to live. Some of the folks who heard me confessing my sins at the revival said I was making up most of it out of my head. Good people would think that. But sinful people like I was didn't doubt the truth when they heard me tell it. The only truth I left out when I was confessing was the names of girls and women I'd fornicated with and I done

[44

that because I didn't want to get shot before I could get home that night.

But getting converted and confessing my sins and then seeing that vision sure changed me from real bad to real good in a hurry. And I ain't done none of them things since all that happened and I can look anybody straight in the face and say how good I am since. But I ain't sorry about my sins after confessing. I figure I know more about sin than most folks and that's why I can preach against it so good now.

I told my wife right after confessing and seeing the vision that I was a changed man and that she wouldn't have no cause to think no more that I was like I used to be. She didn't say much of anything right away, because she knowed all about my fornicating and stealing habits, and I reckon she was just waiting to find out if I was telling the truth or another big lie again.

My wife said she didn't get a vision herself, and maybe didn't need to see one to straighten her out, because I'd never caught her lying and stealing and everything else like I done. She wanted me to stay back up there where all her folks was born and lived, instead of coming down here where there's nothing but strangers every which way she looked. She says she don't feel healthy down here like she did back up there in the mountains, but maybe she'll perk up when she gets more used to it around here.

Right now she's complaining about wanting some new clothes like the other women around here wear. I told her I came down here to North Carolina because the Lord sent me to save souls for Jesus and not go on a dress-buying spree for her. Anyhow, she's a pretty little thing only just twenty years old so far and don't need to dress up fancy like some old women do. Maybe she wouldn't want me to be saying it like this, but, to tell the whole truth about it like I always do now, when she shuts the doors and pulls down the shades and gets herself natural, she's the prettiest little thing of her kind a man could hope to see.

45]

The way I came to find out about this place to preach at here was when I told the preacher back up there at home what the vision said for me to do. He said I'd had the vision just at the very right time, because he'd heard about a new church down here that was an offshoot of another one and it needed a preacher. After I'd told him all about the vision I saw, he said he was sure this was the exact place where God wanted me to come to. He told me there wasn't enough members down here so far to pay me a full-time living but that one of the members promised he could help make up for it by getting me a part-time job in a lumber yard. That suited me because I've been used to heavy work all my life.

Now you see how it came about. And it's working out just like God told me it would in the vision. I've been here a little better than four months now, preaching twice on Sundays and once on Wednesday and Saturday nights in the little church the members put together and I'm winning souls for Jesus Christ all the time.

Folks like to listen to me preach. They like to hear about lying and fornicating and stealing the way I talk about it. One good member told me not long ago he'd never heard a real expert before tell about sinful things the way I do. Sometimes I get to thinking what if I was still back up there where I used to be and hadn't got converted and my soul saved and then hadn't seen the vision to top it off.

When I get to thinking like that, it won't be long till I get down on my knees and thank the Lord for getting me the real religion and seeing the vision. I know there're a lot of other people in the world who go to a different kind of church that don't amount to much, or else they don't have no religion at all, and I feel sorry for all them not being lucky like I was to see the vision and hear God talk to me. That sure was a lucky thing for me. Besides all the souls I'm saving for Jesus, I get three full days work at the lumber yard and can keep half of all the money put in the collection plates on Sunday mornings.

Back up there, before I got converted at the revival, I was working no more than two days a week digging coal for a little company that had a little coal-hole in the mountain near where I lived. Sometimes I could get work only one day a week instead of two, and I never had the chance to share the collection plates at the church. Getting converted and my soul saved and working for God was the best thing that ever happened to me in my whole life so far. And it all happened to me because it started raining and I went inside the church to keep dry.

It'd take a lot of times more than what I'm getting now in cash money to get me to go back to lying and fornicating and stealing and doing all the other sinful things I used to do. And I sure wouldn't want to have to go back working in that old coal-hole and getting all smeared black, neither. Being an evangelist preacher is nice clean work.

I always was a pretty good talker and that's the big thing when it comes to being an evangelist preacher. I always start off talking about the sins I know about first-hand, because people want to know if their sins are about the same or different than mine. Everybody don't sin alike and that's why they want to hear what I done.

After spending the time talking about that, all you have to do next is open up the New Testament anywhere at all it happens to fall open and read off a few words of it.

It all comes easy from then on. I never was much to read much, anyhow, because I never went to school long enough to learn how. But I can always make enough sense out of some of the words in the New Testament to get started. My big trouble after that is slowing down and stopping in time so people won't sit and squirm around on the hard benches longer than an hour, or a little more than that at the most. When I get all steamed up preaching, I never want to quit. It's a natural thing for me to keep on and on.

The preacher back up there who converted me from sin to

salvation and advised what to do about the vision I saw was mighty particular about the kind of Bible to preach with. He made me promise I'd never carry a Bible with the Old Testament in it. He told me why he made me promise that.

He said the Old Testament says nothing much at all about Jesus Christ, which is the way the Jews want religion, but the New Testament does, and that the true religion is out to save souls for Jesus Christ like it says to do in the New Testament. He says the Catholics use a different kind of religion, too, but pay no attention to that and don't waste no time on the other part of the Bible like the Jews do.

That preacher was real smart about religion. He told me that some people don't believe in good evangelism like we do and don't even try to save souls for Jesus like us. He told about preachers in some of the other churches who preach about things you can't even find nowhere in the whole Bible—like about politics and the government and other everyday things. He said it was a pity about having preachers like that around who're not a bit better than the communistic people who don't believe in no part of the Bible at all.

It was a lucky thing for me to be told about things like that about salvation I'd never heard before and could've stayed ignorant about all my life.

Now that I know I've got the true word about salvation and know all there is about lying and fornicating and stealing to start with, I'm satisfied I'm going to be a rampaging, bull-horned, devil-chasing evangelist for Jesus for the rest of my life.

The reason I know that for sure is because it makes me feel so good all over when I stand up there in front of people in church and start working up a sweat no matter what the weather's like. Then when I get to about the middle of what I'm preaching on and the sweat starts running down my skin, nothing in the whole world could make me quit and stop right then.

And then by the time I'm through, if anybody was to ask me, I'd have to tell the truth and say I felt like I was the real Jesus Christ standing there and not just my own self doing all the preaching. That's the true feeling about religion that a good preacher feels deep down inside.

Five

THERE MAY BE SOME evidence of physical and intellectual lassitude among Southern Anglo-Saxon Protestants, but the aggressiveness of their fundamentalistic denominations and the emotional drive of their evangelistic sects are undiminished. Moreover, the memberships of their churches are constantly increasing just as they have been doing decade by decade for the past hundred years. Numerically, they have become a potent force in contemporary American life and, by banding together, their fundamentalistic religious beliefs have already begun to influence a trend towards social and political reactionism.

Understandably, the Negro race in the South, which had always been reluctant to put much trust in a white God or Christ, has little desire for fundamentalistic religion and instead places the greater part of its religious faith in spiritual songs and musical incantations.

As it is, the worship of God among Negroes, no matter how fervent in belief and reverent in attitude, has never approached the religious excesses of white Protestants of the many evangelical sects. And as a result, Negroes are not influenced by fundamentalistic principles in seeking progressive and revolutionary social and political advantages.

There are many reasons for the widespread popularity

of fundamentalism among economically and socially under-privileged Anglo-Saxons in Southern rural regions and factory towns. A listing of them would include the folksy atmosphere of informal religious services, temporary surcease of loneliness, constant reference by the minister to impending death, the promise of instant salvation, a rousing tempo of piano and guitar music, the incitement produced by detailed examples of sexual immorality in sermons, and the opportunity to indulge in emotional spasms in public without inhibition.

The planning and availability of all such church-sponsored activities and inducements are the result of keen competition among numerous fundamentalistic and evangelical sects. The purpose of this is to increase memberships and financial contributions by offering a type of audience participation designed to be more physically stimulating and emotionally exciting than formal and restrained religious services permit.

Neither the agricultural revolution in the South, nor the availability and attraction of drive-in movies and home television, nor the semi-intellectualism of hundreds of yearly graduates of Bob Jones University and other fundamentalistic theological schools, has diminished the appeal that uninhibited religious exhibitions have as popular entertainment to be enjoyed not only on Sunday after Sunday throughout the year, but often on Wednesday and Saturday nights too.

In city and country alike, long-established religious organizations in the Deep South that continue to conduct formal services in an atmosphere of solemn dignity, especially Baptist and Methodist, are constantly being deserted by dissident members who no longer are enthralled and exalted by traditional song-prayer-sermon services.

Many of these are persons who, unless they become religious drop-outs and never see the inside of a church again, will band together to form a more lively religious organization. The more impatient among them will join a sect that has already demonstrated that it encourages uninhibited religious exhibitionism.

What is to the liking of those who reject the formal worship of God, as well as those who object to the intellectualism of sermons concerned with contemporary social, economic, and political matters, are services in which they are given the opportunity and encouraged to participate physically and emotionally. Here uninhibited exhibitions are manifestations of religious faithfulness. The only requirement for being permitted to jump and shout and shake to their hearts' content is the obligation to reconfirm week after week their adherence to orthodox religious principles based exclusively on the literal interpretation of the Bible.

As practised among the sects with relatively large memberships—such as the Assembly of God, the Church of God, the Church of God of Prophesy, the Church of the Nazarene, the Church of God in Christ, Pentecostals, Full Faith Gospel, and Holiness—this fundamentalistic belief instils positive assurance of the virgin birth of Christ, the second coming of Christ, the direct creation of man by God, miraculous healing by faith, the efficacy of prayer, personal salvation of converts and back-sliders, and the reward of physical heavenly existence after death.

It is the weekly celebration of one or more of these fundamentalistic beliefs by a large portion of the Anglo-Saxon population in the South that provides an outlet for various types and styles of religious exhibitionism, which is similar to that commonly associated elsewhere with night clubs and other places of theatrical entertainment.

As in the world of professional entertainment, a variety of acts are performed under the direction of a resident minister or visiting evangelist as master of ceremonies. In churches where this form of exhibitionism is common, four standard acts are performed from time to time.

Ordinarily, only one or two of the acts are presented at each Sunday morning or Sunday evening service. However, during the course of a week-long summer revival or crusade in a tent or church, and on special occasions such as the first or last Sunday of the month, it is usually customary for all four exhibitions to be presented at a single service.

During revivals and on special occasions, there is a standard procedure to be followed when members of a congregation and new converts have been emotionally and physically aroused by the resident minister or visiting evangelist and attain the throes of religious ecstasy. In order that all may participate and find fulfilment in ecstasy, periods of about twenty minutes are allotted for each of the four principal categories.

First, the new converts and old back-sliders leave their pews and go to a position in front of the pulpit to make public confession of their sins and testify to having received salvation.

Second, the church is filled with the resounding babble of glossolalia, or the Unknown Tongue, in an uproar of outspoken individual prayers by the entire congregation beseeching God to grant whatever favour a person desires.

Third, thirty or forty persons move from pews to the kneeling bench in front of the pulpit for the allotted period of loud wailing or silent prayer.

And fourth, the final act and ultimate end of religious

ecstasy and exhibitionism, comes the tearful emotional agony, usually accompanied by violent physical gyrations and jerks, during the progress of 'coming-through', signifying that the devil is being ejected from the body so that the spirit of Christ can enter to bless the soul. As is to be expected among people dedicated to fundamentalistic Protestantism, their extreme conservatism is in keeping with the traditional sharecropper-plantation system, the segregated racial pattern, states rights, and one-party political domination. In both city and country, where such principles have prevailed for generations, the glorification of ruralism and anti-intellectualism is the predominating social, economic, and political influence.

In such an environment, whether in areas of large population or in isolated regions, the solicitation of members for the Ku-Klux-Klan and similar organizations is accomplished with ease. Organizations with a history of terror have a strong appeal for persons prone to cruelty and violence.

The two principal inducements offered prospective members are, first, the opportunity to crusade militantly for the preservation of the white Protestant race and, second, to crusade with evangelical fervour against the implied threat of intellectualism—which is suspected of being in alliance with communism—to abolish the freedom to worship in the accustomed manner in a chosen church.

The Tabernacle of Full Faith in a North Carolina textile town devotes the Sunday night service once each month to a programme of testimonials. The newly-erected brick church has seating space for seven hundred persons and usually on testimonial nights the building is filled to capacity by members and a few curious visitors who come to hear detailed confessions of sin.

The monthly testimonial services are conducted for two specific age-groups which alternate between them. At one service, testimonials are given by boys and girls in the fourteen to seventeen age bracket as a form of initiation into full church membership; at the next service, adult new converts and older back-sliders, who periodically feel the need to confess actual or imaginary sins, are given the opportunity to testify to their salvation.

The trembling dark-haired girl, wearing a floral-print summer dress and white flat-heeled shoes, was sixteen years old and the last of five new members of the tabernacle's Youth For Christ club to give a testimonial. Her father was a textile-mill worker, her mother a restaurant short-order cook, and she had five younger brothers and sisters. She had completed two years of high school when she went to work as a car-hop at a drive-in hamburger stand.

When the girl began speaking, standing below the pulpit and facing the crowded pews, her voice was so low and indistinct that the minister patted her arm comfortingly as he whispered to her. She smiled nervously and began again.

I want all boys and girls to listen to what happened to me. If boys and girls listen to me, they won't get in trouble like I did. That's because they'll learn they'll get in bad trouble like me if they start doing what I did starting about a year ago and doing wrong.

[56

I got in bad trouble doing sinful things. But I'm all right now. Because I quit and Jesus forgave me my sins and saved my soul. I won't never go back to doing bad things again and getting in more trouble. I'm going to keep my soul saved from now on. I promised Jesus I would.

I quit going to school to have a good time and got a job car-hopping. I met a lot of boys and old men. They wanted me to go off with them every night when I got off work at one o'clock. They all had cars and most acted like they had plenty of money to spend.

I wanted to have a good time, but I was scared to go off with them at first. I had a girl-friend at the drive-in who'd been out a lot of times and she said wouldn't much happen if me and her went out on dates together in the same car.

Well, I started doing that and it got so that nearly every night after work I went out on a date at night after one o'clock instead of going home. Sometimes I'd go with the party to an all-night drive-in movie and we'd sit in the car and fool around. Then sometimes we'd just go off somewhere else in the country and fool around.

Then my girl-friend quit her job at the drive-in and left town to go to Charlotte and I kept on going off nearly every night on a date with somebody and me. It wasn't always the same date every time to start with, because dozens of boys and old men kept asking me. Then I got real friendly with one of them and went off with him more than anybody else.

Nearly every time after I started dating him so much I'd get worked up and let him go ahead and handle me like he wanted. He was one of the old men who said he was about thirty-five years old and I got so I liked him so much I'd tell him to go ahead and show me what he wanted. Me and him did that two or three times every week somewhere out in the country in the summertime and then when it turned cold there was a tourist court where we went to for it.

57]

That went on for a long time and I thought sure I was going to have a baby. When I told him about it, he said he couldn't help me none at all because he was already married. I didn't know that. He'd never said so before. Right after that he quit coming to the drive-in and I didn't know how to look him up and I never saw him again.

I was real scared about having a baby and I was scared to tell my folks. I was scared my dad would beat me for it. I kept it all to myself all that time and then found out one day I wasn't going to have a baby after all.

I was so thankful I wasn't going to have a baby that I wanted to pray about it. I'd been to a church some off and on but not much before. But I wanted to pray somewhere. That's why I came in here to the Full Faith church when I was walking by one day and the door was open and I walked right in and got down on my knees and started praying about how thankful I was to be out of trouble.

The minister's wife saw me in here and she got me to tell her all about it. Then she got the minister and he talked to me about joining the church. He said I'd sinned but Jesus would forgive me if I'd repent and say I believed in Jesus. And I've believed in Jesus ever since. Praise God!

That's how I got saved after I'd sinned and now I'm all right. I go home every night now when I finish work and don't run around like I used to. All boys and girls ought to quit sinning like I done and give their souls to Jesus right away. Praise God!

He was a stoop-shouldered man with shaggy greying hair who appeared to be between fifty and fifty-five years old. His tan cotton pants were clean and creased and he was wearing an open-neck summer shirt. He had been sitting in one of the rear pews in the tabernacle and listening intently to the testimonials during the service that had lasted an hour and a half that evening.

Before leaving the tabernacle, he had lingered to shake hands with the minister and had tried to talk to him about something, but the minister shook his head several times as if irritated and had walked away to shake hands with some of the other members.

The man in the open-neck shirt had been among the last to leave the tabernacle, and when he got to the corner, he stopped and looked backwards as though he were reluctant to go off alone and hoped to talk to somebody. It was shortly after ten o'clock on a warm summer night and the street was quiet now that nearly everybody else had left the tabernacle and gone home.

I always go to hear the young folks give testimonials when it's their turn, but none of it's up to what you'd expect these days. I know about that, because it was different in my time. You'd think young folks now would be doing worse sinning than they testify to, but it just ain't so. About all they can say now is they stole something somewhere or told a big lie once or took an auto from somebody to go joy-riding or maybe did a little intercoursing in a motel somewhere. I listen to them every time but what they tell don't amount to much.

Sometimes I get to thinking maybe it ain't their fault for not getting up and telling about the real sinful things they done. I've got a notion it's the preacher's fault for holding them back. He listens to them first in his private room and tells them to leave a lot out when they stand up in front of all the people to testify. He won't let some things be said, because he's holding me back from saying what I want to.

Anyhow, it sure ain't like it used to be. Like it is now, the young folks don't have a sin big enough to boast about. What they said tonight is just like ordinary sin that people do and don't boast about no more. It ain't nothing like I testified about my sins three years ago when I got converted. But to tell the truth, I held

59]

back some myself then because it was my first time and I was a little shamefaced in front of all them people. But when I get a second chance I won't hold nothing back.

What I'm talking about is I'm ready to testify all over again as soon as the preacher lets me. I want people to know what real sinning's like. But the preacher keeps on saying it's too soon yet and wait a while longer to do it again. I tried my best to speak to him again tonight about it and he keeps putting me off and I don't like it one little bit.

The preacher says I'm already saved and don't need to testify again unless I went out and done something worse than I ever done before. Now you can't expect nothing like that of me at my age. And I told that preacher so. Women don't take to me like they used to and sinning with them was the only kind I could ever get interested in. I explained that to the preacher, but he just keeps on saying wait a while longer. Looks like he's ashamed of my kind of sinning and thinks if he puts me off about it long enough I'll get so old I can't remember what I know about it now.

I've been thinking maybe I'll go off to some other church where I'll be appreciated and they'll let me stand up and testify like I want to one more time. I hear the Four Square church wants people like me. They've got sister-preachers, not all men preaching like here in this church, and I've always had a way of getting next to any kind of woman for what I wanted.

That's exactly the sin I want to testify about the next time I get a chance. I didn't mention that main sin the first time I testified about three years ago. I was too bashful about saying it in front of all those strange people. But I'm ready to testify about it now. I told the preacher a little while ago I wanted to testify about sinning with a sister-preacher once, but he made me hush up about it like he keeps on doing all the time.

Anyhow, I only cuddled up with that sister-preacher once and that was a long time ago now. She acted scared and in a big hurry all the time and it didn't amount to nothing much as far as I was

[60

concerned. I quit going to the church to see her preach after that and took up with some married women. There was two of them and that's where some more real big sinning started. That's what I'll testify about the next time if he won't let me testify about the sister-preacher.

Now when you're sinning with two women at the same time, and both of them married, that's when you do the biggest sinning of all. That's got to be true, because it's double sinning and twice as much as ordinary. I told the preacher that over and over again, but he always says wait a while and don't testify about that kind of sinning so soon after the first time I done it.

Like any man knows, and I keep on reminding the preacher about it, when you're dealing with two women at once, you've got to be accommodating to both of them somehow. If you don't, they'll act like women do and one of them is sure to get mad about it and say you're not being fair and square and will start beating on you and biting real bad.

When it all started with those two women, I told them it'd be a lot better for me if they'd let me stretch out the time so I could accommodate one one night and then the other one the next time. But that didn't suit neither one nor the other of them much less both of them. They said they'd always been good friends together and didn't want to split up for favouritism—whatever they meant by saying that. I never was able to figure that out. I guess it must be the kind of talk only women understand.

Just like I told the preacher not long ago, I wasn't used to things like that but I went ahead and done like they said do and that's how I got started sinning double with two married women at the same time.

Now you see why I don't think much of what those young folks testified about in church tonight. If that's all they can confess about, it don't seem like hardly enough to get salvation for.

But I'll tell you one thing. I'm going to keep on pestering that preacher till he breaks down and lets me testify about real big

61]

sins. And if he puts me off too much longer, I'm going off and find me another church somewhere that'll be glad to hear me testify like I want to about that sister-preacher and the two married women. I've got my salvation already and there won't be no need for me to hold back nothing next time.

Six

ALTHOUGH I NEVER HEARD Ira Sylvester criticize another person's religious convictions, he did say once that some unfortunate people, like alcoholics and gluttons, would be better citizens if they could be cured of religious excesses. What he was talking about was what we had seen during a memorable evening in the early 'twenties.

We had been looking through an open window of a country church during a revival meeting on a Saturday night, slapping mosquitoes all the time, while a middle-aged farmer writhed on the floor for about a quarter of an hour and slobbered as though he were having an epileptic fit. This was one of the more violent methods of coming-through and getting religion; ordinarily, participants seeking the same result were content to wail, tremble, shout, and engage in glossolalia. When the man on the floor finally lay still, the minister anointed him with a dab of olive oil on his forehead.

Usually, though, when we went to an evangelistic service at a fundamentalistic church in the 'twenties to observe snake-handling or foot-washing or floor-rolling, exhibitions which ordinarily culminated in emotional shouting and frenzied jumping, Ira Sylvester would come away silent and subdued. It was as if to say that

seeing was enough and that any comment would be super-
fluous.

At other times when I.S. did speak about a particular
service that we had attended, it would often be two or
three days afterwards. More than once his comment then
was that it was a pity religion had been perverted by
certain sects until it had little ethical value left, and was
being used by misguided people for the purpose of in-
dulging in emotional and physical orgies under the guise
of worshipping God.

When I.S. had been particularly depressed by seeing a
minister dangling a rattlesnake above his face or hitting
himself on the head with a wooden mallet, he would say
he wished he knew why stalwart and sensible Anglo-
Saxon people had reverted to such primitivism after only
a few generations in America. He was proud of his own
Scotch-Irish heritage, but he was embarrassed by some
of the religious antics of others of the same Anglo-Saxon
descent.

There were times like this when he would say he was
thinking of resigning from the ministry and would
like to devote the remainder of his life to teaching instead of preaching. There was ample evidence, he rea-
soned, that the South was being engulfed by primitive
religious practices and, in order to counteract their influence, the younger generation should have the opportunity to get a more thorough education in state
schools.

I.S. thought he foresaw from experience that civilization in the South would be retarded for the next fifty or
hundred years, unless the interests of the younger
generations were diverted by adequate secular education
from the pernicious indoctrination of perverted religion.
He said people were going to worship something that

[64

was either spiritual or materialistic and, if they ceased to worship God as a symbol of morality and became addicted to orgiastic religion, the younger generation might be better off being encouraged to worship totem-poles.

At such times as this, when apparently he was on the verge of giving up the ministry, I.S. evidently hesitated to resign because of the still not fully explained reason for his entering the ministry in the beginning. I asked him a second time why he had studied theology and he said no more than he had the first time.

We were driving slowly along a mud-rutted narrow road through flat fields of summertime cotton in bloom. It was several miles from the nearest town and the only houses to be seen were several small, unpainted, tin-roofed dwellings surrounded by bare sandy yards and clusters of green-leafed chinaberry trees. There had been a settlement of Negro shacks and cabins around a cotton gin a mile away, but in the fields the houses were occupied by white tenant farmers.

We had seen nobody in the fields or on the porches of the tenant houses since passing the cotton gin and in the mid-afternoon heat the countryside looked completely deserted. Then suddenly a man, who appeared to be about fifty years old, jumped up from the side of the road where he had been sitting in the shade of a chinaberry tree and began waving his sun-browned, field-straw hat at us.

The excited farmer was wearing once-blue, wire-ripped overalls that had faded almost colourless in the sun and washpot, and his thin face was covered with

65]

a tawny stubble of beard. We stopped as soon as we could and waited for him to come to the side of the car.

Fanning his face with his hat and panting for breath, he asked my father if he were a preacher. We had supposed that he was going to ask for a ride to town and, consequently, it was a surprising question.

When Ira Sylvester said he was a minister, the farmer pointed at the rusty-roofed, three-room house beside the road and told him to hurry. Ira Sylvester asked what the reason was for wanting him to go to the house. Gripping my father's sleeve and urging him to get out of the car, the man said his wife was dying and wanted a faith-healing preacher to lay his hand on her and save her life.

Ira Sylvester told him that he was not a faith-healer and what his wife needed was a doctor. He shook his head and said that a doctor had been there to see her the day before and had told him that his wife was dying with stomach trouble, and that the only way he could help her was to give her some pills to ease her pain. The woman had refused to take the medicine and believed that only a faith-healing Holiness preacher could save her life.

Getting out of the car, Ira Sylvester said he would go to the house and speak to the woman and try to persuade her to take the medicine but that he wanted it understood that he was not going to be able to heal her by faith.

When we went inside the house, a pale, emaciated, grey-haired woman who looked much older than fifty was lying on a soiled bare mattress and was partly covered with an old shimmy-shirt and a thread-ravelled cotton quilt. Hearing footsteps on the plank floor, she opened her eyes and looked at Ira Sylvester with an imploring stare.

He sat down on the chair beside the bed and asked about her illness. After several minutes, when she still had refused to answer any of his questions, he picked up the bottle of pills the doctor had left for her. With a feeble motion of her arm, she tried to knock the bottle from his hand. Then she began begging him to put healing hands on her and make her well.

He spoke to her patiently, telling her that he was a Presbyterian minister, not a faith-healing Holiness, and that he wanted her to go to the county hospital and let the doctors take care of her. While he was talking to her and trying to tell her how much better she would feel if she went to the hospital, she moved closer and tried several times to hit him with her hand. However, each time she lifted her arm, it fell feebly to the mattress.

We had been in the house almost half an hour when my father told her that he was going to have an ambulance come for her and that he wanted her to promise to go to the hospital. Suddenly leaning closer to him, she spat on his face several times in quick succession. As he quickly got up from the chair and wiped the spittle from his face with a handkerchief, she began swearing at him with every curse she knew.

Standing in the middle of the room, he made no effort to silence her. She called him a hypocrite, a fake preacher, a sinful devil, an ungodly Presbyterian, a no-good bastard, a God-damn nobody, a pissing dog, a shit-ass monkey, a son-of-a-bitch, and on and on, over and over again. Then finally, when her husband had tried to make her stop, she began cursing him just as she had cursed Ira Sylvester. Completely exhausted at last, she closed her eyes and lay in silence on the bed.

67]

While we were walking down the path to the car at the side of the road, Ira Sylvester told her husband that he was going to phone a doctor when we got home and have her taken to the county hospital in an ambulance. Jerking the brim of his straw hat over his forehead, and then reaching for Ira Sylvester's hand and shaking it gratefully, he said he was glad to hear that, because he had listened to all the cursing and swearing he wanted to hear for the rest of his life.

We had gone about half the distance home before my father said anything about the dying woman. What he said then was that it was always a sad experience to be in the presence of a dying person, but that he would feel a lot better about it if somebody at the county hospital washed out her mouth with strong soap before she passed away.

I.S. had once said that if all a minister had to do, in addition to living an exemplary life, was to prepare a sermon and deliver it from the church pulpit on Sunday he would have an ideally pleasant and leisurely existence.

What he was talking about was the obligation of the pastor of a church to take part in funeral services and he said that he and the undertaker were called upon to attend more funerals than anybody else in town. Performing marriage ceremonies, however, was always a pleasant task and compensated for all the times he had to go to the cemetery on rainy days in summer and cold days in winter.

No matter how pleasant it had been in the past for I.S. to perform marriage ceremonies, there was one particular occasion when he said afterwards that he wished he had never been called upon to marry a couple.

It was on a winter night between two and three o'clock in the morning when somebody knocked loudly on the front door and woke up everybody in the house. There had been times when somebody was drunk and tried to get into the wrong house, but this time the loud and persistent knocking was of somebody who evidently knew where he was and was being authoritative about it.

I.S. got up, turned on the porch lights and the lights in the living-room, and then quickly came back and put on his shoes and pants and buttoned his coat over his nightshirt.

The first person to enter the living-room was the night-duty telephone exchange operator, a plump woman of about thirty-five with hanging blonde hair, who was rarely seen on the streets or in a store because she slept all day. Behind her came a tall tan-faced salesman several years younger who lived in town and travelled five days a week for a tobacco company. As soon as they had entered the room, a deputy sheriff stepped inside and closed the door behind him. He was the telephone operator's older brother.

The telephone operator and the tobacco salesman, both shivering slightly in the warmth of the house after coming in from the cold, sat down in chairs on opposite sides of the room. Both of them had nodded to I.S. when they came inside, but neither had spoken to him.

By that time, the deputy had already begun telling my father what he wanted done. He was carrying his pistol in a holster on his hip and he put his hand on it from time to time while he was talking. Presently he took a marriage licence from his pocket and said he wanted I.S. to marry his sister and the tobacco salesman right away.

I.S. was wide awake by then and he knew he was not being asked to perform an ordinary marriage ceremony even though he had married runaway couples at all hours of the day and night. The first thing he said about it was, since none of them was a member of the A.R.P. church, it would be better if they spoke to the pastor of the church to which at least one of them belonged. The deputy said he had tried to do that, but a Baptist minister had made the excuse that he had a very bad cold and had to get back into bed in a hurry to ward off pneumonia. He said the other preachers in town were probably not ordained, but he knew I.S. was, and he wanted to be certain the marriage was binding and legal. Besides that, he wanted his sister to be married in a religious ceremony and not by a justice of the peace.

What had happened was that the deputy sheriff's sister had been pregnant for several months and had been able to keep it a secret from him until then, while hoping the tobacco salesman would come back to the telephone office some night and ask her to marry him. When the deputy found out about it earlier in the evening, he had made her tell him who the father was. Acting promptly, he had got the county clerk to go to the courthouse at midnight and issue a marriage licence.

I.S. told the deputy that he would have to ask the couple if they wished to be married before he could perform a legal ceremony and, if either of them said he did not want to be, he would be unable to marry them regardless of the circumstances. Neither the telephone operator nor the tobacco salesman had spoken since coming into the house, and I.S. suggested that since it was so late at night it would be better to wait until morning so everybody would be able to think more clearly about such an important matter.

The deputy sheriff, a stern-faced, heavily-built man in his forties, shook his head determinedly and once more put his hand on the pistol at his hip. He said he was not going to take a second chance on the tobacco salesman leaving town and never coming back again and that he had made up his mind to have the marriage take place there and then.

A lot of time had already passed and the deputy was becoming impatient. I.S. still hesitated, though, explaining that he could not have anything to do with a forced marriage. He said that he would have to be convinced that both of them were willing to be married.

The deputy's sister spoke up immediately and said she wanted to be married right away. There was a long silence while everybody looked at the tobacco salesman and waited to hear what he would say. He glanced at the deputy standing in the middle of the room with the pistol holster hanging from his hip, and then he looked across the room at the telephone operator. After a few moments, he nodded his head with a slight smile.

It was probably one of the fastest marriage ceremonies that had ever been performed, as my father said afterward. And as soon as it was finished, the married couple and the deputy sheriff left the room. When I.S. followed them to the porch, the deputy tried to give him five dollars. I.S. told him to keep the money and use it to help pay for a fine wedding present.

While the bride was getting into the patrol car, the tobacco salesman started walking rapidly down the street alone. I.S. called to the deputy and told him that it was customary for the bride and groom to go away together after the wedding and reminded him that the marriage would not be legal if it were not consummated.

The deputy got into his patrol car and slammed the door. He called to I.S. and said there had already been one consummation too many and that if the tobacco salesman ever came anywhere near his sister again she would be a widow instead of a bride.

Ira Sylvester had been the pastor of the only A.R.P. church in town for about six months when he was handed a petition bearing the signatures of twenty-seven of the more than two hundred members.

The petition of the twenty-seven members was a demand that Ira Sylvester resign as pastor immediately. In demanding his resignation, the stated charges were that he had devoted pastoral time to the affairs of people who were not members of his church, that he had neglected to administer to the spiritual needs of the members, and as a consequence he had violated his obligation to perform the duties of pastor. The petition stated that steps would be taken to have his monthly salary of seventy-five dollars terminated.

Ira Sylvester knew it was a serious charge, but he was not surprised. He had heard that some of the members were complaining that he was not preaching old-time religion and had failed to visit the homes of members on week-days to read inspirational passages from the Bible and pray especially for the soul of each individual.

The comment my father made when he first heard the reports was that old-time religion had been good enough in the past but now should stay there, and that a person who felt the need for daily Bible reading and prayer should learn how to do it himself.

What had instigated the circulation of the petition

by dissident members was that Ira Sylvester was trying to help a destitute white family of man, wife, and eleven children who were living in a three-room shack and adjoining cowshed a short distance beyond the city limits.

The shack had been abandoned by a Negro family earlier that year because a portion of the roof had collapsed and the owner disclaimed any responsibility for making repairs until he could collect rent for it. As it was, the cowshed had a weather-proof tin roof and the family moved to it each time it rained.

Ira Sylvester had tried to get the county sanitation and welfare department to provide a habitable place for the family of thirteen, but the commissioner said that the only duty his office had in such a case was to test the well water used by the family and he would be glad to do that.

The mayor and members of the city council said they had no obligation and no money to provide any kind of relief for people who lived outside the city limits. Ira Sylvester had been able, however, to get a hardware store to donate a roll of tar-paper roofing and several cases of canned food had been donated by some of the storekeepers. At other times he collected wearing apparel from anyone, church members or not, who would give some of their old clothes to the family.

Providing immediate food and clothing for the family had been comparatively easy. What was more difficult was collecting money to pay medical and hospital costs.

The thirty-five-year-old father had lost his right leg in a sawmill accident and needed crutches to be able to walk, and it was not likely that he could get any kind of job until a pair of them could be provided. The six-year-old boy had a broken arm that had not been put into a cast and it was festered and showed evidence of gangrene. The sixteen-year-old daughter of the family had a goitre on her neck that was already the size and shape of a water-dipper gourd and growing larger all the time.

In addition to all that, the thirty-three-year-old mother, who had already borne eleven children and was pregnant again, had begged my father to help her get an operation or some means of birth control to prevent her from ever becoming pregnant another time.

The petition demanding Ira Sylvester's resignation had been handed to him on a Monday. All the other members of the church knew about it by that time, because they had been approached and had refused to sign it, and within a few days nearly everybody in town had heard what had happened. Before the end of the week, two doctors and a surgeon had volunteered their services and enough money was subscribed by citizens to pay all immediate medical and hospital costs for the family.

On the following Sunday morning when Ira Sylvester went to the pulpit, there were more members of the congregation present than there had been at any previous service during the six months that he had been pastor. It was not likely that everybody present took part in what followed, because probably some of the twenty-seven dissident members were there too, but the demonstration was convincing enough of the approval of an overwhelming majority of members. Moreover, there were several non-members present to take part in the demonstration.

Later that day, my father said that it was the first time he had ever received a standing ovation by members of a

church, and his only regret was that when the congregation stood up and applauded him, he should have taken
not one but several bows in appreciation like a professional Shakespearean actor or victorious politician would
have done.

Seven

JUST ABOUT THE ONLY thing many of the Protestant denominations in the Deep South have in common in the 'sixties is the use of the name of God, and even that affinity may not exist much longer.

At the beginning of the present century, methods of religious worship among white Southern Protestants were mostly of the same traditional fundamentalistic pattern. Soon after that, though, a divergence began taking place and once more in the history of Protestantism a definite split occurred. Now in the 'sixties the two extremes have moved so far apart in ideology and practice that there is little apparent similarity between modernism and fundamentalism.

However, even though they pretend to ignore each other's existence, both the modernists and the fundamentalists are well aware that they must, for the present at least, continue to strive aggressively in the name of God for memberships and contributions.

If the divergence continues to widen in the future as it has in the recent past, the use of the name of God may eventually disappear as a theoretical bond between the two practices.

As it is at present, the modernists in many wealthy, urban, large-membership Baptist, Methodist, and Presbyterian churches make use of the name of God sparingly,

77]

if at all, from the pulpit. Some of the most frequently used euphemisms are divinity, spirituality, and ecclesiastic.

It has already become the fashion in some modernist Protestant churches to go through a form of religious devotions without identifying God by name as being the object of worship. Instead of threatening sinners with the wrath of God, a cautious and perceptive pastor will offend no one, and at the same time endear himself to the congregation, by recommending serenity of thought as being the ideal way to obtain a comfortable religious feeling.

Among the fundamentalists in both city and country, however, especially from the pulpits of the Church of God, the Assembly of God, Holiness, and Pentecostal churches, the name of God is inserted indiscriminately, and often reiterated many times over, in almost every spoken phrase or sentence. In fact, anyone not accustomed to hearing such frequent and irrelevant reference to God is likely to be shocked, or at least amazed, and would possibly consider the constant use of God's name to be blasphemy if not outright profanity.

Anyway, when the time comes to decide which of the two factions is to be awarded a franchise, the modernists or the fundamentalists, the latter will have pre-empted the use of the name of God and consequently will be entitled to the exclusive use of it.

Modernist religion in its most advanced form is comparable to the 'boosterism' of such businessmen's civic organizations as Kiwanis, Rotary, and the Junior Chamber of Commerce. Gold stars or enamelled badges are the awards for consistent attendance, vociferous enthusiasm, contributions of money, and volunteered personal services.

Whatever the current objective of a go-getter modernist church may be, buying adjacent property for a parking lot or building an addition for a Sunday-school auditorium or investing church funds in rental apartments, the drive is conducted with the tactics of high-pressure salesmanship. Such campaigns for donations are usually as expertly managed as that of a real estate syndicate negotiating for the development of a new forty-acre, million-dollar, super-shopping centre.

At the other extreme, the fundamentalist church is always poor-mouth. Since financial difficulty is a chronic condition, it is the policy of some of the churches to try to get more money by taking two separate collections at each service—one for the church and one for the minister. Even so, the minister usually has to have a moon-lighting job in a store or filling station or factory in order to support his family.

The reason for such a necessity is that the members of the fundamentalist churches are, for the most part, store clerks, municipal employees, day labourers, and similar wage-earners, and their contributions are not likely to be ample enough to support both the church and the minister. And ironically, as it sometimes happens, when a member becomes relatively wealthy, it is likely that his wife will insist that they improve their social status by joining and contributing to a fashionable uptown Baptist, Methodist, or Presbyterian church.

Just as nothing succeeds like success in any business enterprise, the First Baptist church in a typical Southern city almost invariably has the largest membership, the most imposing edifice architecturally, and the greatest amount of weekly gross income of any Protestant church in town. After it, in descending order come, with few exceptions, the Second Baptist, the Methodist, and the Presbyterian churches. Where there is an exception, it is likely that the Church of Christ will supersede the Presbyterians.

In a Carolina city in the Piedmont that has a population in excess of fifty thousand, the smiling, rotund, jocular, well-dressed pastor of the modernist First Baptist church has little time to devote to the preparation and delivery of sermons in his own church. The reason for this is that about half of his time is spent out of town attending a church convention somewhere in the United States or being the guest speaker at a civic or fraternal banquet in some other Southern city. He is a graduate of the state university and a theological seminary and so far has arranged to receive the honorary degree of doctor of divinity from two Baptist universities and has the prospect of receiving an LL.D.

The enterprising pastor has the services of an assistant minister to preach for him when he is engaged elsewhere, or when he is fatigued after a late evening banquet. The church also pays the salaries of a full-time private secretary for his personal affairs and an office typist for miscellaneous correspondence. He is married, forty-eight years old, and has two sons and a daughter attending out-of-town Baptist colleges. In addition to having the use of a rent-free seven-room parsonage and an automobile furnished by the church, he receives twelve thousand dollars in yearly salary.

The First church is flourishing in every respect to my great satisfaction. I couldn't ask for better attendance and response to our financial needs. Right now our membership is a little more

[80

than a thousand and we are receiving new members every week. Our architects are at work drawing plans for an expansion of the auditorium so that on peak attendance Sundays we can seat an additional two hundred and fifty persons.

But, even before construction begins on the expansion of the auditorium, we've already let a contract to build additional conference-rooms and a larger nursery and a new bassinet-room in our educational wing. And then what we're planning to do next is install a cafeteria for our young people who spend considerable time engaged in their various youth activities during the late afternoon and early evening on week-days in summer and weekends during the school year.

Even while all this is going on, what I have in mind is to raise money to build a complete new wing for a gymnasium and an indoor swimming-pool for our teen-age boys and girls. Our youth should not be deprived of these athletic advantages.

Our programme for expanding our plant and making more facilities available began nearly ten years ago when I took charge of the pastorate. It was my ambition to make the First church the one with the largest membership in the city and to have the most beautiful building of all.

The first step I took was to arrange a fund-raising campaign to buy up all the remaining property adjoining the church so there would be ample space for expansion. As a result of generous donations to the fund, we soon owned the entire block. And then as soon as that was accomplished, I started another money-raising campaign for our building programme. That campaign was pleasingly successful, too.

While it's not of the same magnitude in terms of money, another thing we've been able to do, thanks to the generous response of our members when we asked them to contribute to another special fund, was to buy four complete sets of choir robes so that the twenty-four members of our choir would have a complete change of costume in a different colour for each Sunday

81]

of the month. This created quite a sensation when the newspapers gave us a write-up about it and has resulted in our receiving many new members who transferred from other churches. And besides, this source of money made it possible to offer increased salaries to soloists and other choir members so that we could keep our music department intact.

As to our surplus funds, which come in normally without special solicitation, they are kept separate from our various other campaign funds. We have our investment committee investigating several interesting situations and will soon decide where we will place this money.

Of course, like banks and similar organizations handling large sums of money entrusted to them, our first concern is about the soundness of a long-term investment and our next concern is about the anticipated immediate yield. We operate on the theory that this money should work for us, just as a man does who labours, and we don't want it to get lazy.

It's our general policy to make investments in downtown commercial real estate and in apartment rental units. However, we recognize a promising new trend in property values and we're considering an opportunity to participate in the financing of a large new motel to be built on a main highway just beyond the city limits. Taxes will be lower outside the city and the traffic count on that particular highway makes us very optimistic about the investment.

We haven't reached a final decision yet about the motel investment and I really don't know what the outcome will be. We must keep in mind, as I suppose everybody else in our position does, that housing units for rental to the low-income groups, Negro or white, return about the best yield obtainable these days on per dollar invested. It's unfortunate, considering the people involved, that the percentage of evictions in low-income housing situations is much higher than in commercial and industrial properties. But that's something that has to be taken in stride when you're

[82

responsible for the safety and yield of money put into collection baskets in good faith by the congregation.

As it is, we face these matters squarely and head-on and operate on sound business principles. Since most of our members are well-to-do and many are wealthy, they'd be critical and disapproving if we made investments yielding only the ordinary five and six per cent.

That's why the greater part of our investments are in rental situations in working-class neighbourhoods that give us a return of ten and fifteen per cent and upwards. And, too, that's where we have our best depreciation write-offs for tax purposes, not to mention certain tax-free benefits that only religious and charitable organizations receive. These are features that augment our net income considerably. So you see, it takes good business judgement to operate a church like the First in these days and times.

I'm sure it's because of the success I've had during the past ten years here at the First that I've received feelers from two Baptist colleges in other states. Both of those colleges are anxious to increase their endowment funds and are seeking a highly qualified man to become president and direct campaigns to raise the amounts of money they need. Both of these are challenging situations and I'm going to consider each offer very carefully.

I didn't start out in this field, because primarily I'm a minister, but I've found out in recent years that I do have the ability to plan and direct successful fund-raising campaigns. That's why I'll probably decide to give up my pastorate and accept the best of the two impending offers to become a college president.

I suppose the principal reason for accepting the offer, whichever it'll be, is that as president of a college I'd be soliciting hundreds of thousands of dollars instead of only a few thousand as I do here from time to time. It's my theory that if you hit one bull's-eye, the thing to do is set your sights on another one a little farther away that will bring a bigger reward.

As most ministers will admit, if they're truthful about it, selecting topics for sermons and preaching once or twice a week can become boring and a tedious routine for a man of only average ambition. I'm the kind of person who needs lively action every day of the week and constantly sets himself higher goals of achievement.

You could say I'm not only a go-getter, but also a hurry-upper and a do-it-nower. That's why the challenge of being a college president has great appeal. I'll have a broader field to move around in. I'll be associating with people on a high intellectual level. I'll be in contact with wealthy benefactors. And of course an increase of salary to fifteen thousand, plus an expense account of a few thousand for travel and entertainment, will mean a lot to me. There's no reason why any man shouldn't accept the good things in life when they are put within his reach.

I don't know what the future of religion in America is to be. There'll always be a few of the faithful, I'm sure. Religion is a comfort to the lonely and the bereaved. It provides earthly fellowship. The older generation here in the First are faithful in their duties as members. But the younger generation is becoming excessively interested in the affairs of the outside world and that's why we have to provide more and more activities within the church in order to maintain a hold on them. We must keep them from drifting away. They are the future support of the church.

That's not all that worries us, though. These are difficult times for the young ministers coming up from the theological schools. Most of them think they should jump immediately into the turmoil of the times and this is when they are likely to make their first mistake.

The church today in the South has to play it safe. It is no place for a minister to expound personal convictions when it comes to such matters as integration and racial equality and party politics, or the Ku-Klux-Klan or White Citizens' Council. Secular matters these days are too controversial for the good of the church.

If such topics as these are mentioned in the pulpit, especially by an inexperienced theological student or graduate, and no matter whether pro or con in attitude and inference, there will be some members who will be offended and this would surely result in some degree of dissension in the congregation. The church should be a happy family and not a quarrelsome one. I've worked hard to make the First what it is today. It's a happy family and I want to keep it that way.

I've been very upset about the way some ministers in other denominations have taken a public stand—and have been pickets at demonstrations—concerning civil rights and such matters. It's not a good example for the theological students in our denomination.

This is why I always insist upon reading a young minister's prepared sermon before I'll permit him to deliver it as a guest speaker from my pulpit. There have been times when I've had to blue-pencil almost half of his prepared sermon at the last minute and tell him that he'd have to fill in the interval with a prolonged prayer and additional hymns. Some of them don't like that and will try to argue about it. That's only because they're young and inexperienced. But they'll learn. They'll soon find out they've got to conform to our religious principles.

Like hundreds of other fundamentalist churches in country communities, small towns, and low-income districts of cities in the South, an Assembly of God church was being prepared for the weekly Saturday night, Sunday morning, and Sunday night services. The doors had been closed and locked since the usual service on Wednesday night.

While a small group of elderly women swept the floor and dusted the pews, several young girls were washing the windows. A few men were sitting in automobiles in front of the church and waiting for the women and girls to finish their work.

In the choir loft behind the pulpit, a guitarist and a pianist were practising the scales for some of the hymns the choir director and the minister had selected for the next three services. The energetic young man with the electrically-amplified guitar frequently interspersed hymn music with several bars of recognizable country folk-music and the young woman pianist followed his lead with cautious glances at the elderly women with brooms and dust cloths.

It was a warm Saturday morning in July with thunder-heads moving westerly over the horizon and certain to bring brief showers by mid-afternoon.

The small, wooden, white-painted, unsteepled church, which would seat about two hundred persons, was on a fairly large, sandy, oak-tree lot beside one of the unpaved streets on the south side of the Carolina town. It was a cotton-mill town with a population of almost eight thousand, and the mill itself was within walking distance of the several hundred three- and four-room bungalow-style millworkers' homes that had been built a few feet apart along the unpaved streets. The newly-built Assembly of God church, which was near the centre of the housing, was one of fourteen white Protestant churches in town. The segregated Negro district, which was about half a mile away, had three churches of Negro Protestant denominations.

The minister, bareheaded and wearing an open-neck white shirt, walked down the middle of the dusty street and stopped in the shade of one of the oak trees in front of the church. He was about forty years old with wiry black hair and a lean Anglo-Saxon face. His smile was friendly and he had a strong, moist, clinging, hand-

[86

shaking grip. While he talked he began scraping away with his thumbnail the paper label on a small bottle of olive oil he had bought at a near-by store.

I moved here to town with my wife and family about a year ago. I come from down in the country about twelve miles from here. That's where God spoke to me and told me to come to town and preach the true word of the Bible. I had a little rented farm down there but it didn't amount to much and it wasn't no trouble at all to pick up and leave. I had a good pick-up truck to move furniture and things in.

Well, the way I come to get converted was when I went to a revival meeting near where I used to live and the preacher pointed his finger straight at me and said God was calling me and told me to listen good so I wouldn't miss nothing. And sure enough, I heard God talking to me. I could hear God just as plain as anything. God told me to hurry and get baptized and start preaching as fast as I could.

When I heard that, I stopped to think about it. Me and my wife had been members of a little Methodist church down there for a while, but God told me that didn't count. God said it had to be the Assembly of God church and for me to get baptized in it right away and start all over. Praise God!

Well, it was right in the middle of the wintertime then and hard to get the wet baptism. It was too cold to go to the pond for it, because there was skim-ice on the pond most days then. But the preacher said God made allowance for cold weather in the wintertime. And so the preacher gave me the dry baptism. All I had to do was stand there in the meeting and wait for the spirit of God to get inside me for the dry baptism. If you've ever done it yourself, you know that takes a lot longer than the other kind, because you've got to drive the devil out first, and that ain't easy when you can't drown him under the water and hear him gurgle like in a creek or pond.

Anyhow, about half an hour or so after I got started I started shaking all over and got weak in the knees and dropped down on the floor. The preacher said that was the true sign when you got too weak to stand up. And sure enough right after that I didn't feel the devil in me no more and I knowed God's spirit had got inside me. And it's been in me ever since, too. I can feel the big difference down inside me all the time. Praise God!

The way I do here in town is do both the wet and dry baptisms. In the summertime like it is now I take the young people out to a pond about three miles from here the first Sunday of the month when they're to be wet baptized. It don't hurt them none because young people don't take no risk at all getting a bad cold or pneumonia or something. That's what they mostly like, too, because then they can splash around in the water for a while after it's all done.

But it's different with the old folks. It's too risky giving them the wet baptism. I tell the new converts, if they're old, that they'll have to take it dry and not wet. And I treat the back-sliders the same way when they say they want to get a new feeling of God's spirit no matter how many times they've already had it. Some people will tell you that one baptizing is enough, but I don't believe it, and a lot of good people who come here to church don't believe it. You need another one every time you slip towards the devil and want to get back into God's good graces. Praise God!

Maybe someday I can raise enough money to put in a big water tank in the church and keep it heated all winter long so I can give wet baptisms any time somebody feels the need for it. But raising money ain't easy. It takes time and finding some rich people. I know all about that, because this church can't pay me my whole living. I eke out the rest of the living for me and my family when I can find some hauling to do for a store or somebody with my pick-up truck.

Well, like I said, I don't look for getting a tank for wet baptizing no time soon and that's why I use this little bottle of

[88

olive oil for the dry kind. Some people call it just plain anointing, but I don't. I call it real baptizing.

It takes about a whole bottle a week and it costs a quarter at the grocery store. All it takes to use is one little dab of it on the end of my finger to put on the forehead of somebody when he shakes loose the devil and lets the spirit of God get back in. This is a brand-new bottle now, but by Sunday night it'll be almost gone. That shows how much use I make of it. Praise God!

Eight

IN THE FIRST THREE categories of Protestantism in the Anglo-Saxon South of the 'sixties, the liberals, modernists, and conservatives are fairly well defined and easily identified as Episcopalians, Baptists, Methodists, Presbyterians, and Lutherans. It is in the fourth and final category, which includes dozens of fundamentalistic denominations and sects, that conflicting principles and practices of religious belief constantly create so much confusion and dissension that definitions and identifications are hard to come by.

Among hard-core fundamentalist groups and organizations, such as the Assembly of God, the Church of God, the Nazarenes, the Pentecostals, the Holiness, and the Full Faith Gospel church, there is an ever-present threat of discord and disunity. Even the mention of Christ walking on water or Jonah being swallowed by a whale can quickly develop into an insoluble controversy if it is suggested that such miracles are symbolic and not factual, and will result in a bitter split among the members.

In this highly-sensitive religious atmosphere, disunity will often originate when a minister or praying lay-brother displeases the pew-holders in the Amen Corner*

* Amen Corner: the first several pews in a fundamentalist or evangelistic church, usually in the right-hand corner facing the pulpit. It is a place of privilege for elderly men who demonstrate piety by frequently calling out 'Amen! Amen!' in a loud voice during a sermon.

by failing to stress his belief in Biblical miracles in a voice loud enough to sound sincere and convincing. There is nothing taken more seriously among fundamentalists than the literal interpretation of the Bible.

When such a split does occur in a fundamentalist congregation, and which has not been uncommon during the past fifty years, the immediate step taken by the dissident group is to organize a new church under a different name and become independent of its original denomination or sect.

This proclivity to secede has produced a free-enterprise religious system in which any man can organize a new sect and it accounts for the numerous branches and divisions of a fundamentalist denomination. It also accounts for the fact that some sects reject God and the Old Testament, that some reject Christ and the New Testament, and that others recognize both God and Christ and accept the Bible in its entirety.

What instigates splintering among the fundamentalists is the principle of fundamentalism itself. There is no pope or bishop and no priest or rabbi to issue rules and edicts as guides to belief and to give counsel as to practice. An experienced fundamentalist minister, mindful of his lowly position, will stand aside and be reluctant to favour one faction or the other when a heated controversy is developing.

If the subject is glossolalia, for instance, and regardless of whether he approves or disapproves of speaking in the Unknown Tongue, it is not unusual for him to remain a bystander until the members reach agreement or split the church asunder.

Among fundamentalist sects, each individual acts as his own mentor and, consequently, he strives to attain supreme righteousness for himself by his personal interpretation of the literalness of the Bible. As it often happens, especially in a church where many are uneducated and fanatic, this freedom leads to competition among members trying to prove their claim to righteousness by extreme interpretations of Biblical writings.

However, there is one principal belief that is generally accepted by all: that white fundamentalistic Protestants are God's chosen people and therefore are superior to Jews and Negroes. When this anti-Jewish and anti-Negro doctrine is taught to young people, it is likely to become an obsession as they grow older and result in prejudice, intimidation, and violence.

In the fundamentalist church where the members consider themselves qualified to establish their personal literal interpretations of any passage in the Bible, the minister is always in a precarious position. He is in constant danger of offending some of the members, thereby causing a split in the church or being told to resign. He has to be careful in giving interpretations so they will be acceptable to those who are listening for the slightest deviation from the orthodox and be mindful of the necessity to repeat certain orthodox interpretations each time before leaving the pulpit.

In one instance, after having been forewarned on two occasions prior to Sunday services, a minister who neglected to make the pronouncement from the pulpit that Christ was born of a virgin mother and that God created the earth in six days was charged with heresy and ordered to turn in his key to the church door before leaving town by the end of the week.

In another instance, the ultra-conservative among the members of a fundamentalist church charged the minister with being guilty of heresy when he inadvertently made mention in the pulpit of the earth being round. When he

93]

declined to recant and state that the earth is flat, the dissident group withdrew membership and established a new church in the same neighbourhood that was dedicated to the strict and uncompromising literal interpretation of the Bible.

Fundamentalist preachers enter the ministry with a background ranging from utter illiteracy to university and theological college education and training.

There are numerous theological seminaries, Bible schools, and religious training institutes in the South and elsewhere—the expected large number of them being in the Kentucky and Tennessee foothills of the Cumberlands —and they are graduating hundreds of ministers and evangelists each year upon completion of courses requiring attendance from four years to two weeks. In addition, there are unordained ministerial graduates of hundred-dollar correspondence schools and there are the unordained who said they saw a vision and received the call direct from God to stand up and start preaching.

Of them all, the *élite* among fundamentalist ministers and evangelists are almost invariably those who graduated from Bob Jones University in Greenville, South Carolina. The reason for this distinction is, besides offering a four-year course in theology, expert promotional campaigns have given it the identity of a true university and not an ordinary seminary or Bible school.

Bob Jones University is non-denominational, co-educational, orthodox, Protestant, fundamentalist, evangelistic, and white-only. Its claim to university status— even though it is not accredited by any national educational association—is based on the fact that, in addition to

[94

its college of religion, it also has a college of arts and sciences.

Other than attending required courses in Bible study and evangelism, Bob Jones University students receive practical religious training by attending Sunday-school, Sunday-morning worship, the young people's society, Sunday-evening worship, and daily vespers and chapel six days of the week. All classes, regardless of subject, open with prayer by the professor or an advanced student, and when three or more students meet socially after classes in dormitories or on the campus, they are admonished never to fail to have a 'little-prayer-before-we-go'.

For the more ambitious among the thirty-five hundred students attending Bob Jones University, there are twenty-five extra-curricular missionary, inspirational, and fellowship societies for members of various sects—in addition to Baptist, Methodist, and Presbyterian—such as Christian Alliance, Mission Covenant, Evangelical Brethren, Evangelical Free, and Evangelical Reformed.

The employees in the business office are the appointed spokesmen for Bob Jones University. Professors and students, forewarned and admonished by the administrative trinity—Bob Jones, Sr., Bob Jones, Jr., and Bob Jones III—are not inclined to risk being reprimanded for having discussed with a visitor topics other than prevailing weather conditions and the architectural beauty of the campus buildings.

However, the affable, brisk-mannered young man at his office desk was eager to talk about the success of the university as a cultural centre based on fundamentalistic religious principles.

We've never varied our course to the slightest degree since the original concept of the institution came to our founder, he said.

95]

And our founder, of course, was Dr. Bob Jones himself. In the 'twenties and 'thirties, when Dr. Jones was a famous evangelist all over the South, he had the vision of establishing a great educational institution. And here it is today, just as he wanted to see it, and which we call the world's most unusual university. And why do we call it that? Because it's the one educational institution of higher learning where a young man or young woman can acquire all the essential training needed for an outstanding career in the ministry and evangelism and the missionary field.

Here the student gets full education in the usual college or university courses—fine arts, music, literature, and so on. But—and this is of utmost importance—at the same time he is getting pastoral training and a working knowledge of evangelism while studying theology.

And of course, as Dr. Jones had decreed since the beginning, our emphasis is on fundamental religion. We put special stress on the basic fundamentals, these being the direct creation of man by God, the virgin birth of Jesus Christ, the power of Christ to save men from sin, and the gift of life hereafter by the grace of God.

We take pride in being conservative in secular matters as well as in religious matters. And naturally we teach the dangers of atheism, agnosticism, and scientific interpretations of the gospel. It's for the same reason that we're conservative in political affairs and we show our students the dangers of radicalism and communism so they will be able to work against those forces when they go out into the world. We're confident that when our students leave Bob Jones University they'll know what to vote for and what to vote against. In that way they'll know how to advise their congregations about voting for and against various candidates all the way from local situations to the presidency of the United States.

No, we do not accept Jewish and Negro students at Bob Jones University. That would not be in keeping with our ideals.

It may be surprising to many people to know that our students for the most part do not come from Greenville or the Carolinas.

[96

In fact, the great majority of them come from all over the nation—from New Hampshire to California, from Oregon to Florida. And there's a good reason for this nationwide geographical distribution.

You see, ministers and evangelists all over the country know Bob Jones University because of our splendid reputation even if they've never been students here themselves. They're constantly on the look-out for and recommending outstandingly religious-minded young men and women and often helping them with expenses in practical ways.

For example, a minister or evangelist in North Dakota or Texas or elsewhere will be impressed by the sound religious attitude of a young man who wants to dedicate his life to preaching for God and Jesus Christ and who needs professional training to perfect his talent. As a result, this particular minister or evangelist will stir around and raise enough money to pay the expenses at Bob Jones University for a year. After that, when the young man has proved himself, we'll gladly arrange a scholarship for him or we'll grant him a loan which he can repay over a long term from his future salary as minister or evangelist.

Many people wonder where all the money comes from that enables us to grant scholarships and loans to all needy and deserving students. We got it, and continue to get it too, from the same sources that contributed twenty-five million dollars for us to buy all this land for our campus, erect these thirty magnificent buildings, establish our endowment fund. During his many years as a famous evangelist, Dr. Bob Jones saved the souls of thousands of people and it was in gratitude for this that many of them collected cash contributions for us or remembered us in their wills.

Well, so much money came in and so many students knocked on our doors demanding religious education that we outgrew our small campus in Cleveland, Tennessee, and moved Bob Jones

97]

University to this magnificent large site here in Greenville where we have unlimited space for future expansion. And it's all due to the magnificent crusades of Dr. Bob Jones himself.

You see, ministers and evangelists all over the country believe there's no reason why any young man or woman with the proper attitude towards the religious life as we formulate it can't enrol at Bob Jones University and that's why we have everybody working for us.

Whether or not a student remains for four years and completes his education is up to him. We tell any student to withdraw and leave town if he's not fully and completely co-operative with the spirit of Bob Jones University. We have this policy for two reasons. First, it's for the student's own good. Secondly, it makes room for a student who is co-operative. That's why we're such a happy family of thirty-five hundred students here at Bob Jones University.

Not all of the seventy-five thousand persons living in Greenville are enthusiastic about Bob Jones University. One of the citizens did not hesitate to express his attitude towards the institution. He was a clothing merchant in the central business district and a member of one of the Baptist churches in town. He had been born in Greenville, he had lived there all his life, and his son and daughter were attending the University of South Carolina in Columbia.

We didn't need that Bobby Jay's school here in Greenville to start with and we don't need it now. They pressured dying people to write them into their wills and begged I don't know how many millions of dollars from other people all over the United States so they could move the school down here from Tennessee and put up all those yellow-coloured buildings up at that part of town. And what they've got to show for it is no more of a real university than a Sunday-school class is in a Holiness church twenty miles down the country at a dirt crossroads.

We already had one of the best universities here in Greenville and it still is. Furman is as good a university as you'll find anywhere and all that money should've gone to it. And Furman's only one of a lot of them in South Carolina, too. There's the state university and Clemson and Citadel and Presbyterian and more.

We'd be a lot better off if that Bobby Jay's place had stayed up there in Tennessee instead of moving it down here to Greenville and making a lot of people feel squeamish about living in the same town with it. It belongs up there in the Cumberlands or wherever it was to start with where they'd be with all the rest of the Bible-shouting evangelists. That's about all they teach up there at Bobby Jay's place—preaching, praying, and Bible reading. What kind of education is that for young people these days?

My boy said he wouldn't go to college in that kind of place, and I didn't blame him for one minute. They can't play football, they can't smoke, and they can't look at girls except from a block away. You can't dose food with enough saltpetre to keep a healthy boy's mind off girls. And when they can't find girls, that's when they're liable to get desperate and do something else that's real bad. Now, what man with any common sense at all would make his boy go to a place like that? And it'd be just as bad to make your daughter go there, too.

I don't see many students from Bobby Jay's downtown these days. They used to come down here and pray on the street corners and beg for missionary money. But people got fed up with that and told Bobby Jay's to keep them away. What they do now is keep them up there taking up their time going to prayer meetings and watching the kind of religious movies they show. I don't know where they get their clothes, because they don't buy none from me like the Furman students do. It looks to me like they must be wearing shoddy shirts and pants the school sells them or else they get second-hand clothes shipped from somewhere. One thing I heard about it was that Bobby Jay's wouldn't let students buy clothes downtown because they didn't want any buying done at Jewish stores.

You hear a lot of tales about what goes on up there at Bobby Jay's, but you never know how truthful the tales are because the people who run the school are close-mouthed about what might be a scandal. I've heard about boys climbing through windows in the girls' dormitories and getting caught, but I don't know how truthful that is.

One thing I heard about that was hushed up not long ago up there was about one of the professors and a girl student. That's something that could happen at any school where they try to keep girls separate and I don't see why it wouldn't happen at Bobby Jay's.

The fellow who told me about it is a cabinetmaker who's been doing work up there for several years and he got acquainted with one of the professors who lives on the campus. They got so well acquainted that he'd go to the professor's place after work and they'd sit around and talk a while. The professor was married and had some children. He's been a teacher at Bobby Jay's for four or five years.

Then the last time this fellow went up there to do some cabinet work he found out that the professor had been fired and wasn't there any more. Somebody else who worked up there told him all about it.

The professor who got fired had been fooling around with one of the good-looking girl students and giving her boxes of candy and things like that. He had a little office in one of the classroom buildings and he'd changed the lock on the door and had the only key to it himself. So you know what happened. Just what you'd expect.

This girl got pregnant and it wasn't long before one of the matrons or housekeepers noticed it and made the girl tell all about it. Naturally, the woman went straight to one of the Bobby Jay's and told him all about the girl and the professor.

Well, they shipped that girl home or somewhere an hour later and gave the professor only to sundown that same day to pack up and get off the campus. Nobody knows what his wife did about him, if anything. Anyhow, the scandal got hushed up and only a few people like me know about it.

No matter how you look at it, though, some good is bound to come out of that school up there even if they are overloading the country every year with Bible-shouting preachers and evangelists.

That's why I'll give Bobby Jay's credit for keeping that many boys off the streets at night and running wild on motor-cycles and cars like a lot of others in town do at that age. It's hard on a healthy young boy to get dosed with saltpetre or whatever it is they use on him, I'll grant you. But it does make life easier for the rest of us when they're not trying to run you down with their cars and coming in a store with a gun for a hold-up. And one more thing. It makes things better in town for people who've got young daughters. That's something to be thankful for if nothing else.

Nine

THERE MAY HAVE BEEN other times, and possibly many
of them, but I knew of only one occasion when my father
was so exasperated that he was on the verge of actually
cursing and swearing as certainly many another person
would have done under the circumstances. As it was, he
did a lot of muttering to himself, although he said nothing
out-of-the-way that anyone could hear.

If I.S. had not restrained himself, and had publicly pro-
faned the ministry, he would have had to leave the pulpit
and never return to it. In that case, it would have kept
him from fulfilling his reason for entering the ministry.

However, as he had refrained from doing many times
before when some church matter had been especially
provoking, he did not speak out in a way that would have
made it obligatory as a matter of conscience for him to
resign. Nevertheless, considering what happened, any
minister might have been justified in using any oaths with
which he was familiar.

What had happened that summer in the 'twenties in
the small town in Georgia where I.S. was the pastor of
the A.R.P. church was that the pastors of the other two
churches, the Baptist and the Methodist, had been easily
persuaded by the business manager of a travelling evangelist to agree to co-operate with what was to be a non-
sectarian, interdenominational, Protestant, community

religious revival. The co-operation he wanted was the promise of the three pastors not to hold services in their churches during the evangelistic crusade. The purpose of the revival as stated by the evangelist's manager was to win new converts, inspire good church-goers, and cast fear into back-sliders.

All the merchants in town were enthusiastic about the prospect of having a week-long revival. Some of them who owned clothing stores spoke to I.S. and said they were sure it would stimulate buying of suits and dresses by people who would want new clothes to wear to the services. The owners of the two drugstores said it would be a big help to their business, and even the people who owned the hardware and home-furnishings stores said that a protracted revival in town would bring in better trade than usual for that time of year.

The proposal made by the evangelist's manager was that twice-a-day evangelistic services would be held in a central meeting place and that converts would make their own choice for membership in one of the three Protestant denominations. It was said that the proceeds of the collections would be divided half for the evangelist and half among the three churches.

When he was first approached by the evangelist's manager, who travelled three weeks in advance of revival engagements and made the preliminary arrangements, I.S. said the members of the Associate Reformed Presbyterian church were no better than the members of any other church but that they were already doing the best they could. He said he was confident, if the members of his church needed any additional religious stimulus, that he was capable of providing it for them.

After talking for more than an hour the first time and failing to persuade I.S. to co-operate with his plan for a revival, the business manager left. However, later in the day he came back with the other two ministers. The three of them begged and pleaded with I.S., first stressing the religious need for a summer revival in town and then intimating that his continued opposition would be a retarding influence on religion throughout the whole South as well as making the work of foreign missionaries more difficult.

The final argument of the three men was that the revival, which would be held in the last week of July, would come during the laying-by season on the farms and that that was the only time of year when farmers would leave their crops and bring their families to town early in the morning for the first service and stay late at night for the second service. The business manager had statistics showing that more farmers' families became converts during July than in any other month of the year.

Reluctantly giving in, I.S. told them he was still not convinced by their arguments but, on the chance that there were people in the community who might derive some ethical good from a week of revival services, he would consent to having the A.R.P. church co-operate with the evangelist and the other two denominations.

I.S. then asked to be shown an agreement in writing that would clarify the practical arrangements for the revival.

The evangelist's manager said all of them were good Christians and that it would be an affront to the evangelist as well as to Christianity itself to make arrangements for a religious revival as though it were a common business deal.

He told I.S. that it was customary in the evangelistic field for an experienced evangelist to be given the freedom to conduct a revival as he saw fit so he would be able to

105]

devote all his time and energy to saving souls for Jesus Christ and not have to think about secular matters.

Sometime between midnight and daybreak of the Monday morning in the last week of July, several heavily-loaded trucks arrived in town and were parked on the vacant lot where the revival was to be held. The first service had been advertised to begin promptly at eleven o'clock that morning.

The first people in town to see the big trucks were sure there had been a serious mix-up. Each of the big trucks was painted in bright red, yellow, and green colours with life-size pictures of fat women, thin men, snake-charmers, dancing-girls, and cowboys and Indians.

However, when the drivers and helpers began unloading the trucks at sunup, it was soon evident that they were not setting up a carnival after all.

The men said the carnival company rented the big tent, folding chairs, two pianos, and other equipment to the evangelist and had a contract with him to move everything once a week from one town to the next. They said after they finished raising and staking the rent and setting up the folding chairs and the platform they would leave and go back to Macon and not return until the following Sunday night, when they would take down the tent and truck everything to the next place on the schedule.

The big grey canvas tent was raised and staked by eight o'clock that morning and soon afterward several trucks loaded with sawdust came up the street and dumped their loads at the main entrance of the tent. Several Negro men then began shovelling the sawdust inside and spreading it over the dusty ground.

[106

When the sawdust had been spread, the folding chairs were carried under the tent and arranged in rows with four aisles made for easy movement of people. A wooden platform about thirty feet long and twenty feet deep was set up and bolted securely and then two pianos were carried in and placed near the ends of the platform. The last thing to be brought in was an unusually large and ornate pulpit that had a shelf on one side to hold a water pitcher and glasses.

At nine o'clock several electricians began stringing wires over the platform and from one tent pole to the next and within half an hour the light bulbs had been screwed into the sockets.

All the work had been completed by the time some of the people who had arrived early began going into the tent and selecting the best seats. All the carnival trucks had left to go back to Macon except a small one which had been moved to the rear of the tent but which was still within sight of people walking to the revival. A man and his wife opened the back of the truck and set up a stand that had a red, white, and blue canopy for a sunshade. They were soon ready for business, selling soda pop, hot dogs, and popcorn.

The evangelist, who had reserved all eight rooms on the top floor of the three-story hotel, had arrived in town during the night with the eleven persons on his team. All of them slept late that morning, but, after a quick breakfast at the hotel, they walked the two blocks up the street and entered the tent through a rear flap promptly at eleven o'clock. There were eight hundred folding chairs in the tent and a little more than half of them were occupied when the first revival service began.

The twelve persons on the platform immediately took accustomed positions. The evangelist and his personal manager, who was also the assistant evangelist, sat down in chairs behind the pulpit. Three young girl singers stood at the edge of the platform and behind them were the four ushers who were also singers. The music leader raised both arms, pointing a finger at each of the two piano-players, and the first of four hymns was sung.

As soon as the last hymn was finished, the short, stocky, dark-haired evangelist jumped energetically to his feet and came to the pulpit. He was about forty-five years old and was wearing a baggy seersucker suit and dusty white shoes. Before speaking, he pounded his fist on the pulpit three times and then held both arms above his head while smiling a wordless, open-mouthed greeting to everybody in the tent.

The first thing he said after several moments was that he was going to send everybody home right away to obey God's command to get all their friends, neighbours, and relatives and bring them to the seven o'clock evening service so every chair in the tent would be occupied.

After a significant pause and a profound shaking of his head, he said he had just told a big lie and would have to ask God to be forgiven. Then he announced that before he would let anybody get up and leave they were going to have a friendly get-together so everybody in the tent would be in a happy mood about all the forthcoming days and nights of the week's revival.

This was when he instructed everybody to shake hands with the person on each side of him. While the hand-shaking was going on, he pounded his fist on the pulpit and shouted for everybody to stop.

Covering his eyes with his hands in a shamefaced gesture, the evangelist said he had forgotten that those who were sitting on the aisles could shake hands with only one other person and were being discriminated

[108

against. Beckoning to the four ushers and the three girl singers, he sent them to shake hands with all the aisle-sitters.

By the time the hand-shaking was over, nearly half an hour had passed since the service began and the evangelist sat down and wiped his face with a handkerchief. The assistant evangelist then took charge and motioned to the music leader. First there was a lively piano duet, and then the three girls got up to sing.

The girls were wearing low-cut pink dresses made of voile, so sheer that their black brassieres looked as if they were being worn on the outside instead of inside. The tempo of the piano music increased with each hymn until finally the girls were swaying and waving their arms as though they might switch to a jazz song or country music any moment.

This was when the music was at its highest pitch and the four ushers went down the aisles to collect the offering. The ushers were dressed uniformly in white shoes, black pants, white shirts, and black bow-ties. Instead of carrying collection plates or baskets, they had poles about six feet long and on the end of each was a red velvet bag about the size and shape of a five-pound sugar sack.

The top of the velvet bags had a draw-string opening large enough to receive money but too small for a person's hand to enter. The reason for using such a receptacle was to prevent a person from putting in a half-dollar and taking out a quarter or more in change as he may have been accustomed to do in an ordinary church where collection plates or baskets were used.

When the offering had been collected and taken out of sight behind the platform, the three girls sang one more hymn and then the evangelist stood up and raised his arms above his head while saying a brief benediction.

Immediately after that everybody on the platform hurried through the flap at the rear of the tent and took a short cut to the hotel.

The service that evening at seven o'clock, which the evangelist announced as being the real honest-to-goodness warm-up for the revival, began solemnly with a long prayer by the assistant evangelist asking God to forgive all sinners wherever they were in the world.

The evangelist had changed clothes and was wearing a freshly-pressed white linen suit instead of his baggy seersucker. His assistant and the music leader had changed to dark suits for the evening and all three of them were perspiring and wiping their faces. The July heat was stifling in the tent and people were fanning their faces with hymn-books and anything else they could use.

The three girls, this time wearing thin black voile dresses and white brassieres, sang several hymns and then the evangelist preached a brief sermon describing the beauty of heaven. Nearly all the eight hundred seats in the tent were occupied and it took the four ushers much longer to collect the offering than it had in the morning.

At the conclusion, the evangelist was able to persuade only nine persons to come forward and kneel on the sawdust in front of the pulpit to confess their sins and ask for forgiveness. He quickly accepted their souls for Jesus Christ, and then, his voice trembling, he said he was greatly disappointed that so few had come forward for salvation because he had come there expressly ordered by God to save the soul of every sinner in town.

The evangelist stood at the pulpit in silence for several moments until tears began filling his eyes and glistening on his cheeks in the bright light. After that, he held up his arms while his voice quavered with sobs and said he was so embarrassed for God to know he had saved only nine souls that night that he was going straight to his room in the hotel, get down on his knees, and pray to God to be forgiven for being responsible for such a failure.

Then, leaving the assistant evangelist to pronounce the benediction, he ran across the platform and disappeared through the flap in the tent.

Ira Sylvester had gone to several of the revival services during the week and on Sunday night he went to the final one. Before going inside the tent and sitting in the last row of seats as he had been doing, he went to the refreshment stand behind the tent and bought a bottle of lemon soda and a hot dog.

While he stood there talking to the man and his wife who operated the stand on a profit-sharing basis with the evangelist, the revival services started with loud piano music and everybody else hurried into the tent. The man behind the stand recognized my father and he asked if there had been any accounting and division of the offerings that had been collected during the week. Ira Sylvester told him there had been none yet, but that it had been arranged for him and the other two ministers to meet the evangelist at the hotel immediately after the final service that night.

As it happened, Ira Sylvester never did go into the tent that night. The man's wife began talking about the business practices of the evangelist and how difficult it was to collect what they considered to be their rightful share of profits from the soda-pop and hot-dog concession. She said the evangelist's assistant came to the stand twice a day and took the money in the cash drawer to the hotel without counting it in their presence. She was sure they were being cheated but were unable to do anything about it because they had foolishly signed a six-month agreement that gave the evangelist the sole right to account for the division of profits.

As Ira Sylvester was leaving, the man behind the stand said he hoped the three ministers had an iron-clad agreement that would assure them of getting their honest share of all the money that had been collected during the revival. His final remark to Ira Sylvester was that if they did get an honest accounting they would be doing a lot better than ministers in some other towns in Georgia and Alabama.

After walking around town looking at the three dark churches and listening to the revival music, it was time for Ira Sylvester to go to the hotel. The bright-painted carnival trucks from Macon had already arrived to haul the tent and other equipment to the next town on the schedule and it was about ten o'clock when the revival ended.

The evangelist had hurried from the tent, taking the short cut to the hotel, and he was already upstairs in his room when my father and the other two ministers met in the hotel lobby. After climbing the stairs to the third floor, they knocked on his door.

As Ira Sylvester told about it afterwards, they could hear voices in the room but there was a long wait before the door was finally unlocked and opened.

The bed was littered with scraps of paper and several canvas money-bags were partly hidden behind one of the chairs. Both the evangelist and his assistant shook hands warmly and invited the three of them to sit down. The evangelist, taking off his sweat-damp white coat, smilingly apologized for being in a hurry to pack up and leave for the next town. Then immediately after that his beaming expression vanished and he began shaking his head sadly. He sat down on the side of the bed, covering his face with both hands, and his assistant began reading from a sheet of paper. It was evident right away that no money was to be divided.

After specifying various costs, such as the rental of the tent and other equipment, the carnival company's hauling charges, salaries of twelve persons, rooms and meals in the hotel, and many other items, the assistant said it was regrettable that the receipts only barely covered the expenses. When he finished, he became busily engaged in putting his papers into a briefcase and the ministers were reluctant to question the honesty of his accounting.

Ira Sylvester said that as they were leaving the room the evangelist told them the revival had been a great religious success and he had saved many souls for Jesus Christ and that he hoped to come back the next summer and conduct a crusade that would be a financial success too. Then he said that since he had not personally profited financially, he was sure the three churches would want to pay any bills he had not had time to settle before leaving town. In particular, he hoped the electric company's bill for lighting would not be excessive.

The next morning, muttering to himself with every step, Ira Sylvester walked down the street until he came to the vacant lot where the revival had been held. The only thing that remained to show for it was the trampled sawdust on the ground.

Still muttering, but saying nothing aloud, he walked through the sawdust and kicked at it angrily. When he got to the middle of the lot, he stopped and kicked at the sawdust until he could see the bare ground. This was when he saw a shiny half-dollar gleaming in the sunlight and he reached down for it.

He was still as angry as ever, but he did smile a little when he said that was one half-dollar the evangelist had failed to get his hands on and take out of town. After looking at it for a while, he said he did not need it as a reminder of what had happened and that he was going to let the other two ministers draw straws for it. He said it should serve to remind the minister who won it never to try again to persuade him to agree to another foolish deal with a travelling evangelist.

Ten

I WAS NEVER ABLE to determine the extent of my father's belief, if any, in God and traditional Protestantism, and of course I never asked him about it just as he never asked me about my own belief. I knew by association and observation that he neither practised nor preached what was commonly called old-time religion and it was obvious, perhaps letting his own conduct be an example, that he was giving me the opportunity to form my own opinions about it.

He never mentioned God or Christ to me in private and in the pulpit his direct references to God and Christ were expressed symbolically for the purpose of inspiring ethical conduct among members of the church. Several times he had said that no matter who actually originated or assembled the Ten Commandments—Jews or gentiles, Christians or infidels—no better social code for the ethical conduct of human beings had ever been provided. He said the person who fulfilled these requirements would have to read no further in the Bible in order to learn to be a good citizen.

It was inevitable that such a philosophy as this was going to get I.S. into trouble from time to time with individuals and whole groups in churches where he was either temporary or permanent pastor. This opposition annoyed him and, especially when criticized for not preaching old-time religion, he was usually short-spoken in reply. However, even when it was intimated that his yearly salary of six hundred or twelve hundred or twenty-four hundred dollars might be suspended, he successfully resisted all efforts to make him conform as a minister to certain prevailing practices of Protestantism in the South.

This was during the era when the status of being known as a beloved pastor could be achieved only by visiting members to pray for them in their own homes, unfailingly affirming time after time the literal interpretation of the Bible, and pronouncing damnation upon one and all who differed in religious belief and practice.

Since I.S. made no effort to fulfil these traditional requirements of fundamentalistic Protestantism, and instead devoted most of his time in the 'twenties and 'thirties to some humanitarian project for the benefit of members or non-members, white or Negro, he was at various times accused of being unorthodox. But more than that, it was not unusual for somebody to accuse him behind his back of being guilty of heresy, immorality, dereliction of duty, and being an advocate of racial equality and socialist and communist principles. When he was told of such charges, he said that he might lose confidence in certain fellow men but would always have confidence in himself.

My father's most persistent critics were usually those members of the church who complained that he would always find an excuse not to spend several hours sitting at a family dining-table on a Sunday afternoon and, as he called it, stuffing-the-gullet.

These were frequent clannish gatherings of twenty or twenty-five or more relatives in an affluent family where the customary two- or three-hour Sunday afternoon dinner usually included fried chicken, baked ham, roast beef, hot breads, salads, numerous side dishes, puddings, several kinds of pie, ice cream, and coconut and chocolate cake. I.S. said he had no appetite for such a meal when he knew of dozens of white and Negro labouring families near by having only cornbread and potatoes two or three times a day and that he would have gagged if he had to ask God to bless it.

I.S. probably never used the same blunt language when he declined an invitation to a family meal of that kind, but he did say privately that if he encouraged gluttony by his presence it would mean that he would have to conduct another funeral service and comfort another widow that much sooner.

And then in many churches there was a group of elderly members who had pre-empted the seats in the Amen Corner, and these were the men accustomed to calling out pious exclamations of approval for all to hear when a minister quoted familiar Biblical passages.

When I.S. failed to accommodate the members in the Amen Corner with the expected routine quotations in the manner of old-time religion, giving them no opportunity to indulge in their amen-amen-amen liturgy, it could happen that they would go away from church affronted and disgruntled and pointedly not speaking to him as they left. When they wanted to express complete disapproval of I.S., they would ostentatiously count a handful of coins—sometimes even dollar bills—and then put only a nickel or a dime on the collection plate.

The people in a church I.S. had real sympathy for and wanted to help were those who had become so deeply immersed in religious belief that they had little or no interest in anything else. Almost invariably these were middle-aged or elderly widows who lived alone or had a room with a son or daughter and had lost all desire to take part in ordinary community life. Their only interest seemed to be in reading the Bible and religious publications several hours a day, attending prayer meetings, the missionary society, Sunday-school, church services, and having their pastor sit with them and pray for them over long periods of time several days a week.

When I.S. talked about it, he said these were the most pathetic people he knew and he wanted to do something to help them, even though he knew it would take teams of psychiatrists months and months to wean them from their fanaticism and restore them to normal and useful life. The people themselves should not be condemned for their predicament but ministers and churches should be for having encouraged a socially harmful addiction to religious excesses and should be compelled to do something to cure the victims.

I.S. said he did not think it was harmful for a person to have a belief in God or anything else worthy of veneration as long as he was rational about it and able to recognize and admit the limitations of a belief. What he deplored was the policy of certain Protestant denominations to encourage and even instruct members to go to fanatical extremes as a means of demonstrating their belief in God.

It was his feeling that if such demonstrations were necessary in order to achieve salvation, the members of all churches in the United States should be required to learn glossolalia and the ministers of all denominations should be ordered to practise hitting themselves on the head with a croquet mallet in order to prove that they are sincere about what they preach.

.   .   .   .   .

In the 'twenties and 'thirties in a small town in Georgia, a Protestant minister was frequently called upon to act as a social welfare worker, a marriage counsellor, a financial adviser, an arbitrator between feuding families, a psychiatric consultant, and as a judge to decide what was and what was not moral conduct. Ira Sylvester said he was willing, to the best of his ability, to be a local jack-of-all-trades when necessary, but that he absolutely drew the line when called upon to be a faith-healer.

One of the times my father was severely criticized, not for his attitude concerning faith-healing but for his moral standards, was when a committee of women from the local reading and literary club had gone to the chief-of-police and demanded that he arrest a thirty-year-old divorcee for immoral conduct. As many people in town knew, she had been a prostitute for several months.

The chief hesitated to arrest one woman who lived in the northside residential part of town when several others, both white and Negro, living on the southside had been tolerated prostitutes for many years. Since the young woman was a member of Ira Sylvester's church, although she had not attended services since being divorced the previous year, the chief asked him what he thought should be done.

The chief said that he knew for a fact that some of the husbands of the complaining women had been visiting the divorcee at night, because he had watched her house a number of times, but that as far as he was concerned the men were merely making social calls and no law was being violated. What he wanted to avoid was being forced to raid the house for evidence in order to satisfy the club committee.

Saying that he felt partly responsible for what had happened, Ira Sylvester told the chief that he had heard

119]

rumours about the young woman and should have gone to see her and tried to talk to her about her way of life before the club women made the complaint. This was when he asked the chief to wait a little longer before taking any action and give him a chance to see what he could accomplish.

The chief-of-police was worried about his job, which was an appointed position and which he had held for nearly ten years, and he was fearful of losing it. However, he said he would wait a few more days before doing anything so Ira Sylvester would have a chance to see what he could do. The monthly meeting of the mayor and town council was about a week away and that was when he would have to appear and report what he had done or had not done about the complaint made by the club women.

The good-looking, well-dressed young woman was childless and she had lived alone for nearly a year in a modern brick house on the northside. She had been given the house in the divorce settlement and she also had a small income from a farm. Her former husband had left town and her parents and several other relatives lived in another county.

Ira Sylvester went to the divorcee's house for the first time early in the afternoon. By nightfall, several rumours about his visit were circulating in town. One version was that he had gone to see her in the daytime so it would not embarrass him to be seen there by some of the other men at night. When he was told about this rumour, he said it was partly true, because he had purposely gone there in the daytime so he would not embarrass anybody.

During his visit which lasted about two hours, the young woman, crying part of the time, talked about how lonely and unhappy she was. When she tried to explain why her husband had divorced her, all she could say was that she still loved him and had not been unfaithful during their marriage and that it was her fault for blaming him because they had no children. She said that for a year before the divorce she constantly told him that she would never be happy living with him unless they had children and blamed him because they had none. She said that was the only reason he divorced her and left town.

When he asked her about the rumours that she was entertaining men in her home, she said she did see somebody nearly every night because she was lonely and the women she knew had become unfriendly and that it was the only way she could keep from being miserable all the time. She said that having men come to see her helped a lot but, even so, she often thought about committing suicide. Ira Sylvester said she made no mention of accepting money from men and he did not ask her about it. The important thing to him was to find a way to help her get out of her depression.

He went to see her twice again during the next few days, which caused even more talk about him, including an outright charge of immorality, and by the end of the week he had talked to her former husband on the phone and had persuaded him to come to see her. The only other suggestion made to him was that if they remarried they should lose no time adopting a baby.

Long after they had remarried and gone to Atlanta to live, some members of the reading and literary club continued to criticize Ira Sylvester for what he had done to help a woman who had been a prostitute to remarry her husband and pretend to be respectable. Whatever his thoughts were about the comments, he was content to keep them to himself.

.   .   .   .   .

121]

One of the most difficult situations that confronted my father during those years in the 'twenties and 'thirties came about as the result of the personal conduct of a twenty-eight-year-old bachelor who taught a Sunday-school in the church.

This was another time when Ira Sylvester said every minister should be required to earn a medical degree, or have an equivalent specialized education in a related field, before he was given a theological degree and permitted to assume the responsibility of being a pastor, or else demonstrate convincingly that he was blessed with the wisdom of Solomon. He said again if he could start his life over he would study law or medicine before he would even consider studying for the ministry. And once more there was a strong intimation in the way he talked that he regretted that he had not chosen a profession other than the ministry for his life work.

The young bachelor was a member of a wealthy land-owning family and lived with his parents and an elder unmarried sister in one of the large white colonnaded houses in town. He was tall, handsome, well-mannered and his family took pride in an ancestry that had been traced generation by generation to the early English settlers in South Carolina and Georgia. There were numerous cousins in Charleston and Savannah, and he was a college graduate and worked as a cashier in his father's bank.

His thirty-year-old sister was a college graduate also and had never been married. As brother and sister, and the only children of their parents, they went together to parties and weddings and other social events and every Sunday sat in the family pew in the church.

It may have been different when they were away at college but, as far as it was known, neither he nor his sister had ever had a date since coming home to stay. What baffled some people in town was that the young woman was unusually beautiful and wore fashionable clothes and had a pleasant personality, and yet she evidently had no interest in finding a husband. There had been many times when she had been asked for a date by somebody in town or a visitor and she had always made some excuse for not accepting it.

As for her brother, Ira Sylvester said that he had not thought there was anything unusual about the young man saying he would like to leave the adult Sunday-school class and teach one of several young people's classes. It was arranged for him to take charge of a class for children from seven to ten years old and he taught Bible lessons for about a month.

At the end of a month he said he would rather teach a class of older children. Ira Sylvester asked the Sunday-school superintendent to rearrange the schedule so the young man would be in charge of a class of twelve or fifteen older children. The first Sunday morning when he took charge of the new class, he asked the four girls who had been assigned to it to leave and sit in some other class. No one knew why he had done this but nothing was said about it, and for the next few weeks he taught the class of ten boys whose ages were between ten and fifteen.

It was in the middle of summer then. There was no swimming-pool in town and the nearest place for swimming was at a millpond about four miles away. In the hot weather of July and August many people went to the millpond and often groups would have a picnic supper there in the cool of the evening after sunset.

When the young Sunday-school teacher invited his class of ten boys to go swimming at the millpond on the following Saturday afternoon, all the boys were pleased about it and they had no difficulty getting permission from their parents to go. He arranged to have two cars to take everybody to the swimming party as well as supplying the food for the picnic supper.

All the boys returned home safely that evening and went to Sunday-school as usual the next morning. It was not until the middle of the week, after parents of three of the boys had spoken to my father about it, that he was aware that anything out of the ordinary had happened at the picnic. Then he went immediately to talk to a doctor who was a member of his church. The doctor was a general practitioner, but he was experienced, and he said it was not the first time he had heard of such an occurrence.

This was one of the few occasions, because it was an embarrassing matter to talk openly about at home, when Ira Sylvester did not mention everything he had heard. However, what he left unsaid at home was known to other people who were not so reticent when it came to talking freely about it in the barbershops and some of the stores.

What had happened at the millpond was that when everybody was taking off wet bathing suits and putting on clothes after swimming and getting ready to eat the picnic supper, some of the boys noticed that the Sunday-school teacher was wearing clothing they had never before seen on a man. One of the boys told his father he was so startled when he saw what the teacher was putting on that he thought a girl must have come into the dressing-room by mistake. He said all the other boys noticed it too, but were scared to say anything about it until later when they were alone.

As Ira Sylvester had been told by the three parents,

the young Sunday-school teacher put on women's full-length stockings instead of men's socks and had pink silk garters to hold them up. In one of the barbershops it was said that one of the boys told his father that the stockings and garters looked peculiar enough, but then he fastened a pink brassiere around his chest before putting on his shirt.

At a meeting of the church elders, it was proposed and decided that the expedient thing to do was to suspend Sunday-school entirely and declare a vacation for the remainder of summer until late in September. At that time the Sunday-school was to be reorganized in some manner so that only women would teach classes.

Ira Sylvester said afterwards that his only worry about such a solution to the trouble was that the sister of the young bachelor might say she wanted to take a more active part in the church and insist upon teaching a Sunday-school class of young girls. He said if that happened he was going to revive his interest in going to Africa and be a missionary among the heathen.

Eleven

IN A LARGE SOUTHERN city such as Atlanta it would be unusual if two or more churches of Protestant faith did not have the financial stability of the city's leading banks and the social status of its most exclusive country clubs.

While Atlanta was striving during the first half of the century to achieve economic prosperity and dominance, the Anglo-Saxon Protestants of the city were at the same time industriously building large stone and brick churches with money to spare for architectural grandeur. Now that it has realized its ambition for economic superiority in the South, Atlanta in the 'sixties also has claim to the right to be called a city of grand churches.

Grey stone or mellowed brick, Baptist, Methodist, or Presbyterian, a church in a fashionable neighbourhood—cathedral-inspired in architecture and steepled to high heaven—will be as efficiently managed and as financially solvent as a bank comfortably earning six per cent interest on its loans or the country club with paid-up dues and all bar-chits collectable.

For the wealthy, a membership in one of the fashionable Protestant churches is the best investment in town—tax deductible, with superior business contacts, high rank in local society, and automatic salvation. These are the beautiful people of religion. Country cousins may be members of the same denomination but they live in a

127]

remote world where their church on a weed-grown lot has peeling white paint, unscreened windows, and wasps under the eaves. Destination may be the same but going de luxe is more spiritually comfortable than going second class.

All appears to be tranquil and serene within the financially secure walls of mortgage-free high-church Protestantism, though occasionally there are envious remarks by members feeling twinges of inferiority. This is when pride in their place of worship, no matter how costly and imposing, is moderated by the reminder that ecclesiastical edict gives Catholics the privilege to call their place of worship a cathedral, and restricts others by compelling them to speak of their own architecturally magnificent places of worship in the commonplace terms of church or tabernacle. Truly fundamentalistic Protestants, however, are unconcerned whether Episcopalians call their meeting house a church or cathedral since they are looked upon as belonging to a denomination that expediently straddles the narrow dividing-line between Catholicism and Protestantism.

Spring in Atlanta, when peach trees are budding and millinery is in full flower, is the best time of year to stand aside and watch the Sunday morning fashion parade fore and aft along the route to church.

Then inside the church all will be calm and serene for a precise hour as a religious ceremony is performed with the stylized perfection of a well-rehearsed ballet. Ushers in black suits, the choir in colourful robes, and the minister intoning unoffending platitudes will be aesthetically inspiring to the properly appreciative and solemn-faced congregation.

At the conclusion of the service, another week of salvation will have been assured for all. Then from church door to sidewalk kerb, along the runway lined with appraising young men, the young women with uninhibited spirits have a final opportunity to put their silk-clad buttocks on display.

The well-dressed, college-educated, handsome-faced, Protestant young man had the impressive title of account executive in a stockbroker's office. He was a native Georgian with recognizable Anglo-Saxon features and the nimbleness to be comfortable whether attending a Baptist, Methodist, or Presbyterian church on a Sunday morning. He was still under thirty and unmarried.

Pick out any of these churches in this part of town and it'll be the best place of all to get acquainted with rich stock-buying prospects.

There's something about religion, when you grow up with it in the Baptist church and get to know it like I did, that makes a sort of brotherhood and you don't have to break down doors or get a formal introduction no matter how rich the prospect is. It's like knowing the same language or being an Elk or something like that. I know how it is, because I've worked the night clubs, country clubs, civic clubs, and everything else and I still sell more stocks to people who belong to a high-class church than I do to people I meet in all the other places put together.

The funny thing is you don't have to talk about religion when you get to one of these people. They don't want to talk about that. They put it out of mind as soon as they leave the church. And they don't want to be reminded of it, either. I've been selling stocks for nearly two years now and I caught on to that a long time ago.

Talk about anything else—baseball, football, golf, politics, the governor, Washington—but leave religion and integration alone. You get to talking about integration and segregation and civil rights and such things—and you're dead. No matter how you stand on anything like that, the prospect is liable to blow the top of his head off and you've lost a good chance to get a big account. And it makes no difference if he's from the North or the South—you still don't know which way he's going to jump. These are perilous times in my field and you've got to watch out for your prospect's prejudice.

This's the first time I've been here to this church in about a month. I've got three or four good ones on my list and I alternate. I circulate around because they're good prospects all over this part of town and they're just as likely to be Methodists or Presbyterians as they are Baptists. I tried to make some contacts once in a Lutheran church, and in a Church of Christ, too, but it wasn't worth it. I got nowhere fast. Maybe it's because I grew up a Baptist myself that I can move around better in the big three—Baptist, Methodist, and Presbyterian.

The way I work at it is starting in with the pastor of the church. I don't do that to try to sell him anything. Preachers don't get into the stock market much. For one thing they don't have that kind of money to play with—I mean big money. They like insurance and annuities and their pension funds. That's all right with me if they want something safe and sure like they feel about religion. That's why I never mention the stock market when I talk to a preacher and if he brings it up I always advise him to stay with insurance. Of course now, if I were selling insurance or mutual funds—well, it'd be different.

What I do is go up and shake hands with the pastor as soon as the service is over. They all know me by now and call me by name. Well, I just hang around the minister and wait. There're always a lot of members coming up to shake hands with him and tell him how much they liked his sermon—well, you know how it is. Anyway, it's a natural thing for him to introduce me to them.

[130

I've learned how to size up people at first look and I'll pick out one of them to talk to right then.

I always try to pick out a well-dressed man in his forties or fifties, because that's when they've got money to invest if they're going to have it at all, and he has to have his wife with him too, so I can see how she spends money on clothes and jewellery.

Then if they've got a daughter with them anywhere between eighteen and twenty-five—that's when I say this's for me. I stick with them and leave the church talking all the time about something or other, but I don't hand out my business card then. I want to make the social contact first. I walk with them at least to the end of the block to try to find out what kind of car they drive.

If they've got this daughter with them, then I know I've got a foot in the door. I tell her again what my name is, in case she missed it when the minister introduced us, and make sure of her name so I can get her on the phone. Then I wait a few days until the middle of the week to call her up. By that time I've researched the prospect—I mean, her father—and if everything looks promising, that's when I start working for a date with her.

I like to begin by taking her out to dinner. That's the best way to get acquainted with a girl in a hurry and not waste a lot of time. She's all dressed up and thinking about the kind of moves you might be making. You keep her in suspense by making no moves at all, and that ought to lead to getting invited to her home for dinner or something like that. And that's when you have the opportunity to make the big effort to get on good terms with her old man.

From then on it doesn't always work out a hundred per cent, but I figure on having a fifty-fifty chance of following up and doing business with a prospect I've selected to work on. Anyway, soon after that I'll phone him at his office for an appointment or maybe get him to meet me at a club bar for a few drinks. That's when I hand him my business card and give him a safe and sure tip on the stock market. After that it's win or lose for me with hard-hitting salesmanship. And then if I don't get his account after working like hell for it, I drop him God-damn quick and write him off.

That's my style, because I learned the selling business the hard way. I'll tell you how that was.

Before I got into the brokerage game, I tried other kinds of selling and didn't like anything I had to push. But all the time I liked selling and didn't want to do anything else. When I was in college, I spent a whole summer vacation selling Bibles door-to-door in nearly every little town in Georgia you can think of. I was good at it and I made a lot of money. Anybody ought to be able to do that in this Bible-reading country, but, God-damn it, I ended up hating myself so much I didn't even want to see my face in a mirror. And I even hated the sight of a Bible, too.

Unloading shabby Bibles on poor devils was what did it. I collected two dollars cash down and put the money in my pocket to keep. That was my commission. Then they had to sign up to pay a dollar a month for a whole year. If they missed a payment, the company had a tough two-man crew on the road all the time taking away the Bibles and reselling them to the next poor devils for two dollars and so on.

Those Bibles had blurred print on flimsy paper and stinky imitation leather binding and weren't even worth two dollars to start with. I had two Bibles to sell. One was for white people. The other one was a Black Jesus for the coloured. What the company had done was stick in a few religious pictures and call it illustrated.

Then after I'd graduated from college I got a job selling second-hand automobiles on a big sales lot right here in Atlanta. That doesn't sound like much of a position for a college graduate, but it was available and that makes a difference when you're hungry for a job. I wanted to sell new cars, but the dealer said I'd have to learn the business first by starting on used cars. I didn't mind that at the start much because I was anxious to learn the business.

What I didn't like about that job was finding out I was being a liar and a cheat. I found out that speedometers were turned back to lower mileage and old tyres regrooved to look like new and engines doped to kill the rattles till cars left the lot. Nobody would've bought one of those clunkers if I'd told the truth and keeping quiet made me a liar and a cheat. I quit.

But I still liked selling, and the next job I got was carrying a line of canned goods for a wholesale grocery company. That made me feel a lot better. It was honest salesmanship. My territory was north Georgia and I was on the road six days a week soliciting independent grocers. You don't have a home when you travel like that and it was even hard to get to Atlanta for a night once or twice a month. That's real hard on a boy who likes big city life. So I quit the road after a year and came back to Atlanta to make or break.

I'd taken some business courses in accounting and economics at college, and I'd done that because it's important in big-time salesmanship. So I started looking around. I didn't want a job in a bank or anything like that. That keeps you sitting at a desk. If you're a salesman, you don't even need a desk—you want to get out where you can circulate.

In less than a week I'd heard about a brokerage office that was going to hire a stock salesman and train him for the business. I knew that was for me, and I must've been a good salesman because I sold the boss on giving me the job. That was about two years ago and I'm getting it made.

That's the way it is up to day and date. It was about a year ago when I started the rounds of three or four churches in this part of the city and it's paying off. The only trouble comes when it's time to ease away from one of the young ladies I get friendly with. Some of them get real serious and phone me at home or the office. I try to keep from getting too chummy in a sex way with these girls—unless she's something real special—because that makes it even harder to ease away so I can spend the time on the daughter of another prospective client.

When you've got a list of clients like I've been building up for nearly two years, and don't ease away from all those girls somehow, you're not going to be in any condition to take on new ones when you start a campaign on the next prospects the preacher introduces you to. I've been pretty lucky so far. Most of these girls have gotten married or gone away to college or moved out of town. There are still two or three around that I like to see once in a while, though. They're the special ones I was talking about and are hard to forget.

I expect to be solid in the brokerage business and have it really made in another year and then I can get married and settle down. The way it is now I sure couldn't take on both a wife and all the women I socialize with in my business. When I was selling Bibles and second-hand cars and canned beans, I never thought I'd ever have more of anything than I could use. But that was before I found out what going to church in a churchy town like Atlanta could do for you.

The chairman of the church's finance committee was well-qualified in appearance and ability for an office of such importance. He was in his fifties with greying dark hair and a lean Anglo-Saxon face that was changeably dour and pleasant in expression, and he stood tall and erect with the dignified authority of a successful banker. His position in one of the larger Atlanta banks was vice-president and trust officer. He had been a member of the fashionable northside Protestant church for many years since transferring his membership from a much smaller church of the same denomination in a less prosperous southside neighbourhood.

When a large and magnificent church was being planned to take the place of an older one on the northside, the prominent banker was asked to take charge of the money-raising drive and he had easily succeeded in getting the necessary money over-subscribed even before the ground was broken for the new building. Moreover, when the congregation moved to the imposing new place of worship, he enriched the church treasury by selling the old property for an apartment house site for much more than anybody had even hoped the going price would be. Now, as chairman of the finance committee, he was directing the campaign to increase the church's permanent endowment fund.

The exact purpose of the endowment fund had not yet been stated, but it was assumed that a way would be found to use the income to enhance the beauty of the church and the landscaping of the grounds of the whole square block surrounding it, in the same way that perpetual care is provided by a cemetery.

This is a different kind of money-raising campaign than a church usually undertakes. There is no mortgage on the church and there is no present need to build an addition to it. More than that, we've set no goal to aim at other than to increase the endowment fund. This is so unusual that it creates immediate interest when a person is told about it and that's why we're off and running at the start.

It's a much better plan psychologically than the one used by the Red Cross and Community Chest to get contributions of fixed amounts and for stated purposes. In those drives, there's no element of mystery as to purpose and people will wait and hope their neighbours will contribute enough to attain the goal. That's why such campaigns will lag and then come up short at the end.

The psychological technique we use for our campaign can't fail. We can go sky-high with no time-limit handicap. Otherwise, our campaign workers, being only human, would naturally slacken their efforts when a pre-established goal had been reached. What we're doing is planning the campaign as a long-term drive that's indefinite in time, amount, and objective.

Of course, we accept small contributions—a dollar or two here and there. This gives the smaller contributor the satisfaction of feeling that he's doing his part and we never discourage him. We'll thank him and give him a receipt for his tax purposes. But that's incidental to our main purpose. We want the important bequests —money in the thousands and upwards. These are the kind of bequests we try to get written into wills. That's the real reason we've placed no terminal date on our endowment campaign— we're willing to wait to the end for wills to be probated. Maybe five years, ten years, and longer. It doesn't matter. We're in no hurry. We're content to wait when we know we're going to get a goodly sum eventually.

So far we've had only one bequest contested and the final out-come of that situation won't be decided until there's a court hearing or it's settled to our satisfaction out of court. The four sons and daughters of one of our benefactors have filed a law suit to nullify a bequest to us of several hundred thousand dollars and have begun proceedings to have the court rule that they are to be the sole beneficiaries of their mother's estate.

This was an important bequest that one of our campaign workers spent several months pursuing. Our benefactor was an elderly woman who had been a devoted member of the church for many years. During her lifetime her contributions had been lavish and frequent, and we knew she wanted to make a substantial provision for us in her will.

When the time came to advise her, perhaps our over-zealous campaign worker should not have counselled her to will her entire estate to the church without making reasonable provision for her sons and daughters. But, of course, a will is a will and the law decides.

As it happened, she cut off her four children by willing them only five dollars each from the estate that was worth close to half

[136

of a million dollars. They've gone to court now to attempt to have the bequest to us set aside and petitioned to have the entire estate divided among them. I sympathize with those four descendants, of course, but we have to protect the interests of the church, too.

I don't want to see this go to a jury trial for obvious reasons. The attorneys for the children would no doubt succeed in placing several jurors on the panel who are either members of no church at all—even Jews and Negroes—and consequently would be prejudiced to great extent, or they might be members of some of the smaller churches on the southside and that would have the same prejudicial effect.

We've engaged one of the leading law firms in the city to represent us and we've instructed them to use their best efforts to effect an out-of-court settlement. What we hope to do is settle for half the estate. Personally, I think that's fair to the sons and daughters.

You see, this devoted member of our church had been left this estate by her husband upon his death several years ago and it's not as if she had accumulated it by her own efforts. That's why we convinced her that she should memorialize her late husband by bequeathing it to the church in her will.

But, no matter what turn this situation takes, we have other important benefactors already committed to will to the church substantial amounts for our endowment fund. We couldn't feel any more comfortable about the future.

Twelve

LIKE THE ABUNDANT CROPS of sorghum, corn, and peanuts on the warm moist level-lands, Protestant religion of all faiths and denominations has thrived for generations in the balmy Gulf-breeze climate of south-western Georgia and south-eastern Alabama.

Unlike the uninhibited Cumberland-style fanaticism of the uplands or the sophisticated restraint of big-city, Sunday-only, ceremonial ritualism, this is a region of the Deep South where for more than a hundred years families of English and Scotch-Irish descent have propagated their inherited Protestant religious practices. Now in the 'sixties the folk-ways of the region are so thoroughly imbued with devout beliefs and customs that religious manifestations in secular life are as indigenous as pine trees and drawling speech.

This is where the Bible is kept permanently on view on the living-room table—never closed but always conspicuously opened at a chapter of the New Testament as a constant reminder that it is to be read for daily devotions.

This is where it would be unusual if it were not arranged for a Protestant minister to be present to offer prayer at every type of a public occasion—civic luncheons, fraternal barbecues, homecoming festivals, sports events, and political rallies.

This is where pious customs prevail as inevitably as the daily rising and setting of the sun—grace before meals in public and private, no laughter in the church, tote your Bible on Sunday, and have-a-little-prayer-before-we-go.

This is where the strict code of Christianity is the guiding spirit for personal and business conduct—until the Jew and the Negro presume to intrude socially or economically upon the fiercely-guarded Anglo-Saxon Protestant domain.

White-haired and comfortably fleshy, with a placid countenance and a benevolent smile for all, she was a widow in her seventies with an adequate income from the rental of several dilapidated houses in the segregated Negro section of town. In the warm months of the year, it was her habit to sit in her favourite easy chair on the broad veranda of her daughter's house with her Bible open on her lap and occasionally doze in the cooling Gulf breeze of a summer afternoon.

She lived with her married daughter in the one-story weather-greyed wooden house on the quiet tree-shaded street and had been a life-long member of the gleaming-white, high-steepled church only walking distance away at the end of the block. Unfailingly carrying her Bible, she walked to the church and back in pleasant weather. On rainy days and in the cold weather of winter her son-in-law took her in his car to the church door twice on Sunday and to the weekly Wednesday night prayer meeting.

Her pew in the church was on the centre aisle in the second front row and, unlike the other pews, it had been fitted with a seat cushion by the young pastor for her comfort during the services that ordinarily lasted an hour and a half.

It was her custom to arrive at church at least half an hour early and she always lingered for another half an hour or longer after the services to talk to the pastor and some of the other members. This was when she took delight in chiding the young minister by telling him that she was more religious than he was because, by spending a total of five hours in church at morning and evening services on Sunday, an hour on Wednesday nights, and two hours daily reading her Bible at home, she devoted a greater amount of time to religious observance than he did. He always nodded gravely and patted her hand in penitence.

I get so much comfort from my religion and I just love my wonderful pastor. He's as saintly as the day is long. When people tell me how well and happy I look and compliment me that way, I always tell them I have an even better inner feeling because I read my Bible every day and love my pastor so much.

Every morning when I wake up and every night before I go to sleep I pray to the Lord to bless my pastor and keep him in good health and let nothing evil happen to him. It'd break my heart if anything evil happened to him or if he lost his health. I've outlived two of my pastors and I know what sorrow it is to have my pastor pass away. I pray to the Lord every day that when the time comes for one of us to go, this time I want to go first and not be left behind.

My pastor is a fine upright young man and I want him to be here so he can preach my funeral service when the time comes. I've already told him what passage in the Bible I want him to read at the service. That's why in all my prayers I pray the Lord to bless him with good health and long life.

My biggest sorrow about my pastor is that his wife is a simple

141]

*little thing and nowhere near good enough for him. He deserves a
finer wife and that's why I have such a big sorrow. It's awful that
a good man like him has to bear a burden like her in life.*

*When I sit in my pew at church and look up at my pastor, I
feel so sorry for him that it makes me want to do something for
him to make up for him being married to a plain little thing like
her. She sits there in the front pew and I feel like ordering her out
of the sacred church for pretending to be so holy-minded when she's
nothing but a common little thing.*

*Then when I send for him to come visit me and read the Bible
and pray for me, I can't keep from letting my tears flow when
I have to think about him leaving me and going home to her. I
make all the excuses I can think of to keep him with me as long
as I can. It's awful to have to think about him going home to
that pitiful little thing and being there alone in the parsonage
with her.*

*Ever since I saw them together the first time about four years
ago when they moved here from Macon, I've felt sorry for him and
wanted to do something for him. She's so plain-looking and so
unsuitable for a fine-looking man like him. I tried once with all
Christian charity, but I couldn't see anything to praise her about.
She doesn't know what to do about her clothes and she can't fix
her hair and I just know she's going to ruin his health with her
awful cooking.*

*I'm sure as anything that a fine man like him never would've
married a miserable little thing like her if she hadn't done something awful to get him to marry her that no decent woman would
do. There's a lot of contemptible females in this world who have
no shame at all about such things and she's certainly one of them.
She doesn't fool me for one minute with all her pious looks, sitting
there in church pretending to look like an unsullied angel.*

*If he'd only come here a single man to be our pastor before she
did something awful to get him to marry her in Macon, I could've
put a stop to it. I know all about her kind and I would've saved*

[142

him from her clutches. She's not the first back-alley slut I've seen in my life.

Well, thank the Lord, they don't have any children and they've been married four years and I hope and pray they never do. It's so mortifying to have to think that a fine young man like him would have to humble himself in her presence for intimate bodily relations with a common little thing who'd have no shame at all about what she did to entice him. I weep every time I think about him doing such a thing over there in the parsonage with her.

I don't believe in divorce, because the Bible says it's evil, and so what I do is pray for my pastor to be strong and high-minded and not humble himself in her presence. If my prayers are answered, he'll stay pure and won't humble himself. The Bible teaches that the Lord looks with favour upon a good man who keeps himself pure when tempted by evil. It won't be easy for him living under the same roof with her, but he knows I pray for him and he says my prayers are a great help and comfort to him.

I love my pastor so much. And I feel so sorry for him. That's why I pray for him night and day. And I just know that my prayers will be answered and he'll be delivered somehow from the temptation to humble himself in her presence. Maybe her health will fail and she'll pass away soon.

There were several barbershops in town. The largest one of them, which faced the courthouse square, had four chairs and was the favourite of out-of-town visitors and high-school boys who patronized it because the barbers were young and sophisticated and would not cut off too much hair. All the others were one-chair, non-union, owner-operated shops.

Almost everybody else patronized the one-chair barbershops on the side streets, not only because haircuts were twenty-five cents cheaper, but also because there was more freedom to talk about what was happening in town and

143]

tell all kind of jokes when schoolboys and strangers were not present. Even if they did not want haircuts, there were usually two or three or more men sitting in one of the small barbershops since it was a good place to talk and pass the time.

The plain, resin-beaded, pine-boarded walls of the one-chair barbershop, which was a block from the courthouse square, were covered with dozens of large pictorial calendars and colourful pictures that had been taken from men's magazines and religious periodicals. In the helter-skelter array on the walls were Babe Ruth and Joe DiMaggio in baseball uniforms, Red Grange and Charley Conerly in football gear, Barry Goldwater and George Wallace in speech-making action, girls in exotic nude poses, and blood-dripping pictures of Jesus Christ crowned with thorns and nailed to the cross. On the rear wall, and isolated from the other pictures, was a large photograph of white-robed men marching in a torchlight Ku-Klux-Klan parade.

The tall, solemn-faced barber was slowly and methodically trimming the sandy-coloured hair of a middle-aged man in pale blue coveralls who worked in the gasoline filling station on the other side of the street. When the customer came across the street and sat down in the chair, he had casually asked what had happened around town over the weekend.

The barber began talking about a meeting he had attended the previous Saturday night in a pasture about three miles south of town.

It was a fine night out there for a meeting. The weather cleared up just before sundown after that thunder shower we had in the afternoon and a good moon was out. When the rain first started coming down Saturday afternoon, I thought to myself, Oh God,

[144

we're going to get rained out again like it was a couple of weeks ago when we set up the meeting out there.

You remember that time. There'd been a two-inch rain that day and that pasture was as mucky as a God-damn pig-pen. You couldn't expect people to go out there and stand around in that mess. But it was different last Saturday night. There hadn't been much of a shower, anyhow, and the footing was nice and dry. You couldn't ask for it to be better, by God.

By eight o'clock last Saturday night, I'd estimate there was about two hundred people out there in that pasture right behind that old barn on the Howard place. I counted more than fifty cars and pick-up trucks strung out along the side of the road when I got there and there must've been nearly that many more by the time things got started a little before nine o'clock.

We had a fine speaker who'd come down from Montgomery, but before that we started out with a little talk and a real fine prayer by that preacher here in town you know about who always shows up for a meeting. It's too bad you had to work that night at the gas station and couldn't get off work for it. You missed a God-damn fine meeting.

Well, like I said, the meeting started off about nine o'clock like we wanted. It was light enough by the moon for it then and all the people had got there. When the preacher finished up praying, then this fellow who'd come from Montgomery took charge of things from then on. I'd heard he'd run other meetings before in Alabama and Georgia and down in Florida and other places and he acted like a God-damn expert.

The main thing he said at the start was we ought to come out in the open more in the daytime and show ourselves around and don't be bashful about it. He said the civil rights law makes the niggers get bolder all the time and it's up to us to draw a line somewhere and keep them from crossing it. He said the way to go about it is let it get printed in the newspapers and told on the radio that we're going to keep niggers in their place and then if

145]

some of them make a move to cross the line the thing to do is go out there and by God shove them back where they belong.

He said you let the niggers get the least bit of a toe-hold and after that they'll try to move next door to you and want to sit beside you in your own church. Then he said watch out for the Jews, too, because the Jews ain't on our side and they'll go right along with the niggers and try to move in and take over from us.

What he talked about next was about the demonstrations the niggers put on and he said we can outnumber them two to one any time we want to and told us to get out there and do it the next time they tried to put on a demonstration about something. Then he ended up saying we ought to have more meetings like that one Saturday night because the niggers hear about it and that lets them know we mean business and by God no fooling. He passed out a little sheet of newspaper to everybody telling what's being done about the niggers all over the country and showing how to go about handling them when they get out of line. It was a real educational newspaper to read.

It was almost eleven o'clock by then and it was time for the meeting to break up and that's when the cross was lit. It sure made a pretty sight when it blazed up. It stood about twelve feet high on top of a mound in the pasture and the cross-piece was maybe four or five feet wide. It'd been soaked in gasoline I don't know how long and then wrapped around with cloth. It was made out of two-by-fours to make it burn longer and it lasted a good whole hour.

People started leaving before it was all finished but some of us stayed till it was all burned out because we didn't want no wind to come up and blow sparks across the pasture and set fire to that old barn. It wouldn't do to let that happen so some folks could accuse us of barn-burning when we're out to do good and not no harm.

I don't know when the next meeting's going to be, but you be sure and fix it up so you can get off from work the next time and

[146

be there. By God, you wouldn't want to miss two big sights like that all in a row.

It was the last remaining general merchandise store of its kind in town and it had been family owned during the seventy-five years of its existence. The store was in a good business location on one of the corners of the courthouse square. The spacious red-brick building was only one story in height, but its elaborately-designed wooden scrollwork front extended another two stories above the ground floor. It was as much of a landmark as the tall, belfry-topped, yellow-brick courthouse in the centre of the square.

The merchandise on display on the time-scarred counters and shelves—family clothing, dry goods, furniture, and hardware—was in a jumble of disorder with pots and pans intermingling with baby cribs and bolts of cloth. Just the same, the balding, florid-faced, sixty-year-old grandson of the founder of the business and his two elderly clerks could immediately put their hands on any called-for item if it happened to be in stock.

However, the complaint of the owner was that he was steadily losing trade and would soon be forced out of business by the discount prices and flashy window displays of competing chain stores, variety stores, and specialty shops. He said he was going to do his best to hold out for another year or two, though, before being forced to sell out and see a new owner modernize the store and stock a different line of merchandise.

I've been a faithful church member and a good Christian ever since I was baptized when I was a young man nearly forty-five years ago. My wife's just as good a Christian as anybody else, too, and she spends all her spare time working for the missionary society and helping to raise money for the Christian cause all over the world. But I can't understand what got into our three children. They were raised in the Christian life like anybody else. I had Bible reading and prayer for them every day of the week besides the Sundays. But they just didn't have interest in the church like me and my wife and it wasn't long before they married and moved away from town.

And it wasn't only the church. They didn't want to work in the store and learn the business so they could keep on running it for another family generation after I'm gone. They acted like they was ashamed to work in the store and when something was said about it they'd say it was too old-fashioned for them to work in. I know that much about what they said about the store, but I never was able to pin them down about what they had against the church.

When I see one of them now and then and bring up the subject of their church-going habits, they won't say exactly yes or no about it and I can't be sure they've kept on going to church after they left home. It looks to me like they're trying to keep from hurting my feelings about not going to church.

I told all three of them I've provided enough family burial space in the churchyard cemetery for them and their families, but they don't even want to be buried anywhere near the church. All that hurts me, like it does them not wanting to work in the store and carry on the family business when I'm gone.

Well, that's how come I'm here all by myself without my children helping me run the store and keeping the business in the family. Now, I don't have nothing special against the Jews, except they ain't like us, but some of them moved in here and opened up a big store across the square over there selling just about what I do except furniture and hardware. They stocked everything in their store top to bottom from hats to shoes for the whole family right down to baby clothes.

Then on top of that they advertised discount prices on merchan-

[148

dise 'way down below what I charged for the same item and sometimes cheaper than I could get it wholesale. That was about two years ago when they started that. And ever since every time I lower prices on something, they cut their selling prices down under me to draw customers and they don't think nothing of knocking something off that mark-up to make a sale.

I'd heard about the Jews before, but I didn't think much about it till some of them came here to town. And what the Jews done about cutting prices under me was bad enough, but even that wasn't the worst of it. You know what else they done? Well, I'll tell you.

You know what the custom is. When one of the coloured comes in the store and asks to buy something, you hand it to him and he pays for it and then he walks out. I've done business like that with the coloured all my life. They knew they couldn't come in here and try on clothes, because if something didn't fit after that and they didn't buy it, it'd be spoiled for white customers. The only exception was I'd let them try on shoes before they picked out a pair to buy.

Now here's what happened. Since the Jews opened that store across the square, black niggers can walk in there and try on any clothes they please. And the Jews who run the store will even unlace their old shoes for them and sit down in front of them and help them try on all the shoes they want till they get the fit they want to buy. Ain't that something?

Well, I'll go bankrupt and get put out of business before you see me squatting down in front of a black nigger, lacing and unlacing shoes for him like he was a white man.

I'm a good Christian and I'd get down on my knees and wash the feet of Jesus Christ if I had the chance. But you'll never see me getting down like that in front of a black nigger and tying his shoe laces for him. But the Jews will do it, because they're Jews. That's all need be said about it.

Thirteen

I.S. SAID HE GREW UP on a North Carolina farm where anybody who ploughed with a Tennessee-bred mule, especially in stumpy new-ground in the heat of summer, learned early in life all the locally-known expletives that were necessary for proficiency in the occupation of farming. And, more than that, a ploughboy soon became proficient in devising new expressions and exclamations of his own to use in the presence of a balky, stubborn, oath-provoking mule. He said after that he had never heard anybody demonstrate being capable of contributing much to the vocabulary of cursing and swearing.

I knew of few times when I.S. became offended or embarrassed or protested the vulgarity and blasphemy of others in his presence by calling attention to the fact that he was a minister. Usually, by silence and displaying a lack of enthusiasm, by appearing to be bored by the absence of originality in a turn of phrase, he soon made even strangers realize that their swear-worded language was not appreciated.

It was as if I.S. were saying that every person had a right to express himself as he wished, but that the conversation would be a lot more interesting to him if so much time were not wasted by digressing from the subject to make scatological reference to God, Jesus Christ, and the Virgin Mary.

After mules, the stubbornness of early models of automobiles to perform and the hazards of pioneering in horse-and-buggy country provided the logical transition of swearing language from farm to city and highway. However, whether kicking a mule or a car, the invectives were the same.

Long before the First World War, my father became interested in automobiles and the first one he bought was a 1909 model Ford. Thereafter, whenever a later model was put on the market, he was quick to trade his old car for a new one.

I.S. still travelled in those days by train when time was short and the distance great, but there were many trips to near-by places he could take in a car and sometimes in summer he drove from one state to another in it.

One of the difficulties about automobile travel then was that the dirt roads were muddy and slippery in winter and either deeply rutted or boggy with sand the remainder of the year. And there were times when the radiator sprang a leak or the drive-shaft broke and he would have to spend hours or days making repairs by the side of the road. This meant that he was not always able to keep an appointment or deliver a sermon. When he was delayed too long, he would have to turn around and go back home.

However, even when roads were passable and no break-downs occurred, there was always the possibility that a horse would shy at the sight of an automobile and upset a buggy and anger the people riding in it. This was not uncommon and it sometimes resulted in arrests and threats of law suits.

.   .   .   .   .

One of the longer automobile trips we took, both in distance and in time, was from the Carolinas over the Blue Ridge Mountains to northern Virginia. I.S. was going to take charge of an A.R.P. church in Virginia for a year and, since it was summertime and he had just bought a newer model Ford, it was a good opportunity to take a long trip in a car. There was plenty of time for the trip and he did not have to hurry to get there.

The longest delay during the whole trip occurred high in the Blue Ridge when we travelled only six miles one day from early morning until long after nightfall. The reason for this was not because the car broke down or due to road conditions but because I.S. said he was thirsty and stopped to ask a black-bearded man sitting on a log beside the road where he could get a drink.

The mountaineer told I.S. to follow him and they disappeared into the woods. It was at least two hours before they came back and this time I.S. was walking in front and the man with the black beard followed with his rifle pointed directly at my father's head. There was not a word said when he reached the car and it was plain that the man was angry about something. He ordered I.S. not to crank up the car and try to leave until he said he was ready for us to go.

After a long wait, a horse and buggy came down the road with the driver using a whip on the horse. Just before they reached the car, the mountaineer jumped up and waved his arms excitedly. The horse shied instantly and ran off the road into a ditch with the buggy tilting on its side.

The driver, who was a boy about seventeen years old and who had the appearance of being the mountaineer's son, jumped from the buggy and held the horse by the

153]

bridle while the older man talked to him. After that, the boy uprighted the buggy, whipped up the horse, and drove down the road as fast as the horse would go.

Still not speaking to I.S. but keeping the rifle pointed at him, the mountaineer sat down again beside the road. After about half an hour, he stood up and told I.S. to crank the car and drive away.

There was no opportunity for I.S. to explain all that had happened and what the trouble was about, other than to say he never did get a drink of spring water, because we had gone less than a mile when we came to the first houses of a town and in the middle of the road stood several men with rifles blocking the way. When we stopped, one of the men showed I.S. a sheriff's badge and said he was under arrest for shying a horse with an automobile and causing a buggy to upset. One of the deputies rode on the running-board of the car and we drove into town and stopped at the small, red-brick courthouse in the centre of the square.

I.S. posted a bond, which he expected to forfeit, as did everybody else in the courthouse, and we drove slowly out of town in low gear so as not to risk being arrested again for scaring a horse or speeding. It was very late in the afternoon by then and it was dark before we found a farmhouse by the roadside where we could get something to eat and spent the night.

My father said the whole trouble had started when they got to a still in the woods and the mountaineer became angry because he insisted that all he wanted was a drink of water and did not want to buy a gallon jug of moonshine corn liquor. After the moonshiner had lowered the price in order to sell a jug, and I.S. still refused to buy it, he told I.S. to sample the liquor by taking a free drink. When he declined, the moonshiner became even more angry

[154

and affronted and began cursing him for refusing to accept the hospitality.

This was when he made I.S. go with him to a house near by where his son was sitting on the porch. I.S. said he had not been able to overhear anything, but that evidently this was when the boy was told to hitch a horse to the buggy and drive down the road to the automobile. At that 'time the horse was to be shied and then the boy was to drive to town and tell the sheriff to arrest I.S.

As for what else had happened during the two hours he was at the still and out of sight, I.S. said he had tried to convince the moonshiner that the reason he wanted a drink of spring water and not moonshine whisky was because he was a minister. The man had said that my father did not look like a preacher to him and was probably a government revenue agent trying to find the location of the still. This was when he began swearing and using expressions that I.S. said he had not heard since leaving the farm.

I.S. said he began talking fast at that point in an effort to prove that he was a minister, and probably made the most convincing religious appeal to a sinner in his life, because he had heard of government revenue agents being shot on the spot when they discovered the location of an illegal corn liquor still. He said he did not mind the moonshiner retaliating by having him arrested for scaring a horse with an automobile because it was a small price to pay as ransom for his life.

And as for the next trip over the Blue Ridge, he said that he was not only going to carry his own drinking water with him but also wear a clerical collar so he would not be exposed again to the vulgar and blasphemous language of a mountaineer that might be suitable for

155]

government revenue agents to hear but not for a minister who had left the farm a long time ago.

It was a custom on country roads in the early days of the automobile for the driver to take it for granted that the right of way belonged to him when meeting a horse and buggy or a team of mules hitched to a wagon. The custom originated, in South Carolina anyway, for two practical reasons.

For one thing the roads were usually only one-car wide and, more importantly, it was wise for buggy-riders and farmers in wagons to leave the road and drive into a field where they had a better chance to control their horses and mules and keep them from shying and bolting at the sight and strange sound of an automobile.

This was a sensible custom for farmers for their own protection, but as the number of automobiles increased, a motorist often assumed that when he met another car on a narrow road that he alone was entitled to the right of way. However, for many people, it was the customary courtesy of the road when two cars met in a single lane for one of the drivers to take it upon himself to back to the nearest wide space and give the other driver the right of way.

Nevertheless, there were times when two motorists met on a narrow road where both stubbornly insisted upon having the right of way and neither would back up his car. This was when arguments could develop into fist-fights.

I.S. had started out early on a warm Sunday to drive his car from Prosperity to an A.R.P. church near Newberry where he was to preach during the eleven o'clock morning service. The distance was less than ten miles

[156

and he had estimated that it might take as long as an hour or an hour and a half for the trip.

It was midsummer in South Carolina and the road was dry and dusty, although portions of it were either deeply rutted or boggy with sand and only one-car wide. As usual when the roads were dusty he wore his linen duster over his good suit of clothes.

We had gone about half the distance in our new, cream-coloured, three-seater Ford, which had a double seat in front and a single seat on the tool box in the rear, when we came to a portion of the road that was wide enough for two cars to meet and pass without either of them having to stop. This was where the road, instead of being boggy with sand, had two deep ruts in the hard red clay.

When two cars met at such a place, it was easy enough, if both drivers were courteous, for them to pass without even having to slow down. All that was necessary at a time like that was for each driver to steer his left-hand wheels into the right-hand rut. However, once the driver had steered into both of the deep ruts, it was impossible to get the wheels out of the ruts and he would have to back up and start all over again.

We saw a car about a hundred yards ahead that was coming towards us at a fast rate of speed and my father immediately steered his left-hand wheels into the right-hand rut. There was plenty of time for both cars to get into the proper ruts for passing and he assumed that the other driver would do just as he had done.

The other car came straight ahead, using both of the two ruts in the road and not slowing down at all. When I.S. saw what was happening, he put on the brakes and stopped as quickly as he could. The other car then began slowing down, but it did not stop until its left front wheel had hit our left wheel with a jolting bump.

The automobile that had run into us was a large, black Pierce Arrow that looked like a limousine and there were two other men in it in addition to the driver. All three of them were wearing dusters, two of them sitting on the front seat and one in the rear, and they got out immediately and walked towards us.

One of the men began talking in a loud voice and accusing I.S. of failing to get out of their way. I.S. said nothing in reply and the angry man began cursing and swearing at him. While that was taking place, a heavy-bodied, scowling, red-faced man began impatiently pacing up and down the road with his long linen duster flapping around his legs.

The man who was doing all the talking and cursing asked I.S. if he knew whose car he was obstructing by not getting out of the way. I.S. said he recognized the governor in the long duster but, no matter whose car it was, he was well on his own proper side of the road and was not at fault.

I.S. got out then to see if the front axle of our car had been bent when we were hit by the other automobile. He decided that no damage had been done and he stood aside to wait for the governor's car to be moved out of the way. It was long after ten o'clock by then and there was not much time left for him to get to the church to preach.

The governor was still walking up and down along the side of the road and taking no part in the argument. The other man continued swearing at I.S. in a loud voice, but my father only shook his head from time to time and made no reply. A horse-drawn buggy came up the road with people in it who evidently were on their way to a near-by church, and then a second buggy got there. Both of the drivers, seeing that the road was completely blocked, started through the field in order to get around the two cars. The governor waved to the people to stop and then went out to shake hands with them.

I.S. got back into our car and sat down at the steering-wheel to wait. It was long after eleven o'clock when the governor came back at last after talking to the people in the buggies and, since it would have taken at least half an hour to drive to the church from there, I.S. said it was going to be the first time he had failed to appear at a church where he was expected.

The governor had found out that I.S. was a minister when he talked to the people in the buggies and he hurried to our car and shook hands with I.S. for a long time. He was apologizing and saying how sorry he was for what had happened and offering to do any favour I.S. would ask.

My father told him that the best favour he could do was to tell the man who was cursing and swearing to shut up and back the big car out of the way. By the time that was done, it was useless for us to go any farther. We sat there and watched the governor's car back up, drive around us with wheels in the proper rut, and then disappear down the road in the direction of Columbia.

There was a place not far away where we could turn our car around and start back to Prosperity. We had gone about two miles on the way home when I.S. said that the Sunday had not been wasted after all because at least the governor and two of his staff had been given a good opportunity to learn to respect the courtesy of the road. If he decided they had learned something, he might even vote again for the governor at the next election.

I.S. said that in his opinion the soft, grey, dirt roads near the Mississippi River in Tennessee were the most

159]

hazardous for automobiles of all the roads he had known anywhere in the South. Even the main roads often were flat on the rain-soaked earth without gravel topping or drainage ditches, and the year-around rains kept them deeply rutted and miry with grey mud.

When portions of the roads were not flooded by heavy rains, they became dangerously slippery even after a brief shower in summer or winter. Everyone in our neighbourhood who owned an automobile also kept a horse and buggy to use in the worst of weather. Moreover, a horse was necessary at times for pulling a person's car out of a mud-hole in his own driveway or when it skidded off the road after a rain.

Our house was close to the main road through Tipton County where we lived about midway between Covington and Memphis. Like others who owned an automobile, we kept a horse and buggy to use when it would have been foolish to try to go somewhere and back in our 1913 model Ford. My father sympathized with people in cars who got stuck in the mud on the road or turned over at a slippery curve, but he said that it would not be long until farmers got tired of hitching up a team in the middle of the night when somebody was in trouble and often only receiving a few words of thanks for their help.

It was between one and two o'clock at night after a heavy shower in the middle of March when somebody knocked on our door and asked I.S. to help him get his car out of a mud-hole. I.S. got out of bed and told the stranger that he had no team to hitch to a car and that one of the farmers near by might be able to help. The stranger told I.S. he had already tried to get help at two farmhouses and nobody was willing to do anything for him at that time of night.

The man began begging I.S. to help him in some way

because he was in a big hurry to get to Memphis before daylight. My father asked where he came from and why he was in such a hurry to get to Memphis, but all he would say was that he had started from Kentucky that afternoon.

We went to the barn and put the plough collar on the buggy horse, got the trace chains, a single-tree, a heavy rope, and then went up the road about a quarter of a mile to where a big dark-coloured car had skidded axle-deep into a mud-hole.

The night was starry, though not bright with moonlight, and it was easy enough to see what we were doing. With the horse pulling and everybody pushing, we got the heavy car back to the road. We had not seen what make of automobile it was, but it was big enough to be a limousine.

The owner of the car handed I.S. ten dollars, but my father said he was glad to be of help and needed no pay. Even though he insisted, saying the help was worth every penny of it to him and would gladly pay more, I.S. still declined to take the money. When we were ready to leave, the man opened the rear door of the car, reached under a tarpaulin, took out two large bottles of whisky, and handed them to I.S.

We watched the heavily loaded car go cautiously down the muddy road towards Memphis until it was out of sight and then we walked homeward with I.S. carrying the two bottles of whisky. When we got there, we put the horse in the stall and left the bottles on the corn-crib floor in the barn.

On the way to the house to go back to bed, he said he had never given aid to a bootlegger before in his life but did not regret it because it was the only time he had ever been around a man who did not curse and swear a blue streak when he was having car trouble.

Fourteen

AS SECRETARY OF THE home mission board of the A.R.P. synod, Ira Sylvester was accustomed to dealing with religious and secular matters that caused conflict and disunity within a congregation. Having had many years of experience in the field from Virginia to Florida and Florida to Tennessee, he was well qualified for such a responsible position.

Among his qualifications was a forthright way of expressing his religious views and personal opinions concerning the welfare of the church. Calm and objective, his outspokenness did not always endear him to everybody in a strange place or even in the community in which he lived. And as for his personal life, he was unconcerned about public opinion and made no excuses for his own principles.

As the result of his frank way of speaking from the pulpit and on the street, Ira Sylvester was frequently criticized by members of his own church as well as by members of other denominations who mildly disagreed with him or who became grossly offended. When criticized mildly, he would be called unorthodox. When criticized severely, he was called irreligious and, if the mood were bitter, atheist and communist.

It was not that Ira Sylvester took delight in controversy or encouraged and purposely instigated it. What happened

163]

was that he was characteristically not conservative in opinion and was unconcerned about unfavourable reactions once he had definitely decided what to do for the good of the church or for a cause which was secular and not religious in nature.

He riled many people, as a result, who had been conditioned by a provincial environment and intellectually retarded by inadequate education compounded by religious fantasy. When he took an unpopular stand on a controversial matter or did not side with an individual whose point of view was unacceptable to him, he would not express disdain for anyone but would say that the younger generation would be more fortunate in being able to receive educational advantages the older generation had been denied. This did not mean that he thought he was always right and never wrong. When he realized he had made a mistake, he was quick to admit it.

The tragedy of religion in the South, as Ira Sylvester said when depressed by the prevalence of fanaticism, was that glorious races of people—Scottish, Irish, English, Huguenots, and others—had been fortunate in finding a Protestant haven in the United States and then, unfortunately, had permitted the practice of their religion to become debased and perverted. He never said that religion itself was at fault. He blamed it on the lack of adequate education and the failure of the ministry to provide intelligent guidance for many generations.

As he saw it, exultant Protestantism in the South had degenerated into excessive emotionalism—which was the glorification of religion for religion's sake—and that all ethical values inherent in the Bible were ignored and replaced by the theatrical antics of evangelism and the mesmerizing promises of spirituality and immortality.

[164

The loneliness of existence in the agricultural South, the human yearning for a better life after death, the excitement of the crowd at a Sunday meeting, and the suave persuasion of evangelism was a combination that rarely failed to produce an abundance of emotional and physical ecstasy.

It was this long-term trend in Southern life and its inevitable consequences—the exultation of fanatical religious practices ranging from snake-charming to head-pounding to blood-letting—that influenced my father in making his long-deferred and final decision as to the way he would devote the remainder of his life.

It could not be said that he had failed as a minister—it was that the religious practices that prevailed in some Protestant churches had been less than an ennobling influence on people and consequently had brought disenchantment to him.

Ira Sylvester's assignments had usually lasted from six months to a year, although that was before he became pastor of an A.R.P. church in west Tennessee. The difficulty within the congregation kept him there for all of three years. When he finally resigned as pastor, he said it had been the most difficult task he had ever been called upon to perform.

To begin with, it was one of the larger churches in the synod with a membership of several hundred and also one of the most prosperous and financially secure. As it happened, the wealthiest members, who controlled the treasury and all church finances, organized a dissident minority group for the purpose of withdrawing the church from the A.R.P. synod and becoming affiliated

165]

with another Protestant denomination that was extremely fundamentalistic in practice.

In order to accomplish this withdrawal, all members who did not side with the dissident group were discouraged from attending services in the church and, if they persisted in attending, they were pointedly ignored and treated with silence.

The reason given by the dissident members for attempting to take the church into another denomination was the charge that the A.R.P. ministers were too intellectual and impersonal and failed to preach old-time religion. Several ministers had resigned after a few weeks for various reasons and the most recent one to resign had left because the agitating group had removed the authorized psalm-books from the church and replaced them with hymn-books.

When Ira Sylvester arrived to take charge of the west Tennessee pastorate, he immediately had the unauthorized hymn-books removed and replaced with the psalm-books of the denomination. In retaliation, efforts were made to provoke I.S. and bring about his resignation too.

A series of provocative acts began when a petition was circulated by the dissident members demanding that he resign because he had failed to preach the true gospel and instead had devoted his sermons to secular matters. When the petition was presented to him, he found that it had been signed by less than a third of the membership. In rejecting it, however, he offered to resign if the full membership voted in person either by a show of hands or by ballot and a majority went on record as not wanting him to continue as pastor. The petition was withdrawn and no membership meeting was held.

Several months later the next effort was made to force him to leave. His salary was reduced by half by the

[166

treasurer with the explanation that contributions were not sufficient for full payment. This scheme failed when loyal members stopped putting money into the collection baskets and contributed the other half of his salary directly to him.

During the following year, numerous other schemes were complete failures and Ira Sylvester thought he had succeeded in his task to unify the congregation and was ready to resign and go elsewhere. However, this was in the middle of the participation by the United States in the First World War and the dissident group found one more opportunity to harass I.S.

Ira Sylvester used patriotism in time of war as the theme of a sermon and this was the cause of a series of retaliatory acts that continued for an entire year. He had to put aside for the duration of the war his plan to resign.

First, there was a whispering campaign. Put into circulation was the charge that my father was being paid by an unidentified subversive organization to encourage Protestant white boys and men to volunteer for the armed services so that they would be sent to Europe to be killed and that Negroes and Jews would be spared so they would be able to rule the country.

The effect of the whispering campaign against Ira Sylvester prompted him to devote a whole series of sermons concerned with patriotism. In retaliation for this, a nightriding campaign was organized for the purpose of intimidating young men who were planning to volunteer for service in the army and navy. And in addition to that, government recruiting posters were torn down and burned within a few days of being put up in public places.

He persisted in extolling patriotism Sunday after Sunday until he was visited by nightriders who advised him

167]

to leave west Tennessee immediately. He ignored the warning until finally he began receiving threatening letters in the mail and written messages of threat were left at the front door of the house. He did not report the threats against his life, but he did notify the nearest recruiting office that government posters were being burned. That brought a quick end to the harassment that had lasted a year and he was never threatened again.

At the end of the First World War, he decided that he had served both his country and his church and that he could leave west Tennessee in good conscience. He resigned as pastor of the church and as secretary of the home mission board and said he looked forward to another way of life elsewhere. However, he was still an A.R.P. minister.

We were at this small town in the farming country of southern Alabama in the late summer when the heat was not too uncomfortable. There was usually a brief shower in late afternoon and then the nights would be clear and starry. The flies were big and lazy by that time of year, but the mosquitoes had a sting that would itch all night.

The religious revival in the big brown tent was advertised on placards that had been tacked to telephone poles, fronts of vacant stores, and any other available space. It was to last for an entire week, morning and night, and the evangelists were husband and wife who employed a music leader who had an accordion as an accompaniment for audience singing. There was no door charge and contributions were solicited at the beginning and again at the conclusion of each meeting by the

[168

husband and wife who carried large wicker baskets through the aisles while the accordionist played lively tunes.

The revival was an independent enterprise of the two evangelists and was not associated with any local church. It was advertised as being interdenominational and the implication was that a person with membership in any church was obligated to attend all services in order to maintain his religious standing. Some of the stores in town closed in the morning so clerks and owners could attend and then at night people from miles around came to the service.

This was not one of the primitive religious exhibitions that were common in the Deep South in the 'twenties where an evangelist would ram his head against the pulpit or draw blood from his arm and smear it on his face or drain blood from a chicken and drink it. Just the same, my father had heard about the crusading style of the husband and wife and he wanted to see how they conducted one of their revival meetings.

The wife on the evangelistic team was the first to speak from the platform after the opening collection had been taken. She was a stout woman who appeared to be about thirty-five years old, with hanging yellow hair and wearing a clinging black dress, and she moved with energetic leaps from one end of the platform to the other while begging and imploring everybody in the tent to get ready to dedicate his soul to Jesus Christ. She perspired freely in the heat of the night and she would stop in the middle of a sentence to wipe her face and neck with a small towel that hung on a nail at the side of the pulpit.

Her inspirational talk was a brief summary of her life before she was converted to Christianity at a similar revival meeting in Mobile. She said she had lived for the devil by coveting the fine clothes and pretty jewellery of other women until she thought money and property were the most important things in life and that this had led her to the extreme limits of sexuality. In closing, she said she was unable to say more about her life of sin when men were present but that she would be glad to talk to young girls and women of all ages in private at the conclusion of the service.

We were sitting near the rear of the tent and I.S. was already squirming on the hard seat of the backless bench by the time the husband on the team took his place at the pulpit. The evangelist had a large Bible in a bright red binding which he stroked and patted affectionately as he looked from one side of the tent to the other and smiled at the audience of about three hundred persons.

His wife had sat down on a chair at the rear of the platform and she was fanning herself energetically as she talked in a confidential manner to the music leader beside her. During the silence at the pulpit, she whispered something to the music leader and he quickly covered his mouth with both hands when he began laughing.

The evangelist at the pulpit was a tall, thin, solemn-faced man of about forty who was wearing a black suit, white shirt, and a black bow-tie. He had a thick fringe of brown hair and the dome of his head was completely bald and shiny in the bright light.

The first thing the evangelist said was an order for everybody in the tent to bow his head and pray in silence for exactly one minute. After that, slapping the big Bible with a resounding thump, he told everybody in the tent who wanted to be saved by Jesus Christ and go to heaven to stand up and let it be known that he was eager to receive salvation.

I.S. stood up as everyone else did, and then he kept

on moving towards the nearest exit of the tent. We got outside to the weedy lot just as the evangelist began recounting the story of his sinful life prior to the time when he received salvation at a similar revival. As we stood there, his voice became louder and rose to a higher pitch. There were several other men near by in the semi-darkness and they would listen for a few moments and then talk among themselves about what they had heard the evangelist say about his sins.

Presently one of the men asked I.S. if he were going back into the tent when the call came for everybody who had sins to confess to go to the platform and receive salvation. His answer was that if he had sins to confess he would prefer to wrestle with them in private rather than in public.

As we were walking away, one of the men remarked loudly enough for I.S. to hear that there went a poor devil who evidently was loaded down with so many bad sins that he was ashamed to confess them in public, and was going to lose the only chance he might ever have to get salvation.

Immediately following the end of the First World War and well into the 'twenties, east Georgia was gripped by a craze for the game of baseball and the fervour for the game was as evident among spectators as it was among players. There were regions in the South other than east Georgia where the craze was rampant; however, it did not seem likely at the time that there could have been more feverish baseball activity elsewhere than there was in the numerous small towns in the counties of Jefferson, Washington, Glascock, Burke, and Emanuel.

There was no organized league of semi-professional teams, but that was of small matter because rivalry was so strong between teams and the partisanship of fans was so emotionally expressed that each game was played as if it were a crucial contest in one of the major leagues. The most intense competition was always between teams representing closely situated towns where the population had been previously conditioned for rivalry by years of high-school baseball and football competition.

The difference was that semi-pro baseball was played by men for money and not by boys for fun and the good of the game. It was inevitable under these circumstances that sometimes there would be fist-fights in the stands and on the playing field and that umpires would be assaulted and had to be escorted out of town. This was why extra police with pistols and truncheons would always be on duty at the baseball park to try to maintain order and prevent serious physical injuries. When a fight-minded fan was blackjacked, handcuffed, and taken to jail, he would be released after the game in time to go home for dinner.

There was excitement for everybody at a semi-pro game—even for the scorekeeper. Being the official score-keeper for a season for the games played on the home field of one of the Jefferson County teams provided immediate excitement when a visiting player was charged with an error or not credited with a hit and the decision was posted on the scoreboard on the centre field fence. If the offended player became enraged and ran off the field towards the scorekeeper's bench—grabbing a bat from the bat-boy on the way—the police protection was comforting.

During the baseball season from April to the end of September when I was scorekeeper and statistician for the Wrens semi-pro club, it was customary to schedule at least one game a week to be played on the home field and preferably on a Saturday afternoon. During the final month of the season, a second game would be scheduled for a day in midweek.

In the final month of the scheduled games there were few persons in the whole town who appeared to be unconcerned about the wins and losses of the local team. It seemed as if everybody—druggists, storekeepers, mail carriers, delivery boys, garage mechanics, and even some doctors and dentists—wore a baseball cap as evidence of loyalty to the home team and as a way of expressing enthusiasm for the sport.

Even though my father did not wear a baseball cap, he attended most of the games. In addition, he was a member of a booster club that had been organized for the purpose of raising a fund that would give each player a bonus at the end of the season. The booster club had little difficulty in collecting the needed amount of money from enthusiastic businessmen and doctors.

After that, however, instead of disbanding the booster club when its original purpose had been fulfilled, some of the members began making sizable bets with fans of teams in Louisville, Sandersville, Swainsboro, Waynesboro, and other near-by towns. When I.S. heard about it, he promptly withdrew from the club.

All the men in the booster club were members of one of the several churches in town. Some of them were elders or deacons and all had strong religious convictions. As it happened, considerable amounts of money had been pooled and bet on one of the final games of the season. The night before the game was to be played it was rumoured that the visiting team had acquired the services of a high-priced pitcher who had pitched a no-hit game the previous week for one of the other east Georgia semi-pro teams.

It was too late then to hedge bets and some of the booster club members were so worried about losing their money that they came to see I.S. late at night. What they asked him to do was to go to the dressing-room of the local team just before the start of the next day's game and pray for the players to win.

I.S. said it was one of the most irreligious requests for prayer he had ever heard. Then he told them that he was not even going to the baseball park to watch the game because his presence might be interpreted as approval of the betting by some booster club members and it might be thought that he was silently praying for them to win their bets. As they were leaving, he said he did not wish them any hard luck but, if they lost, it might be the end of what had become a gambling club.

The next day's game was won by the visiting team and the men who had lost their bets said I.S. was to blame for what had happened. Those who talked about it for several days afterwards said they were convinced that he had silently prayed for the visiting team to win so they would lose their money. When told about it, I.S. smiled but had nothing to say.

Fifteen

AFTER NEARLY TWENTY-FIVE years of service as
secretary of the home mission board of the A.R.P. synod
and having been temporary pastor of numerous churches
throughout the South, Ira Sylvester said the time had
come for him to fulfil a cherished lifetime ambition. In
the past he had often been on the verge of resigning from
the ministry but he had never before come so close to
doing so.

This was in the early 'twenties. The plantation system
was flourishing, but not for the economic and social
benefit of uneducated and under-privileged white and
Negro share-croppers and wage-workers. By this time
Ira Sylvester was more convinced than ever that adequate
education would be the only effective means of helping
to alleviate a human depression in the South that religious
practices of many Protestant denominations had either
condoned or ignored. It was this desire to take an active
part in the education of the school-age generation that
brought about his decision to become a full-time teacher
in the public schools.

In order to become qualified and proficient as a teacher
with a master of arts degree, Ira Sylvester planned his life
so that he could devote a total of two years of study first
at Columbia University and finally at the University of
Georgia.

Perhaps he was honouring a pledge he may have given his mother, or perhaps it was a means of partial financial support, but whatever the reason, he accepted the permanent pastorate of a church of his denomination in Wrens, a small town in east Georgia near Augusta. During the next several years, by obtaining frequent leave of absence as pastor and earning money for some of his university expenses by working as an editorial writer for one of the Augusta newspapers, he completed the requirements for a master's degree at the University of Georgia.

First as professor of English in Wrens high school and later as teacher of science and history, this was still not enough to fulfil Ira Sylvester's concept of adequate education for high-school students. Believing that scholastic study should be balanced with physical training, he organized the school's first athletic department and, in addition to his classroom duties, coached football, basketball, baseball, and track teams. It was not as if he had had no experience as an athlete. In addition to playing baseball, he had been centre on the football team at college in the days when there were twelve players on the squad—eleven to play the game and one to sit on the bench as a substitute in case of injury.

Even though his duties as a full-time teacher for five days and athletic coach for six days a week left only Sundays for him to act as pastor of the church, he received no complaints. More than that, the members approved when I.S. told them that if he could not provide all the needed religious inspiration during a Sunday morning service, then he felt it would be useless to try to make up for his ineffectualness by having Sunday-night services and Wednesday-night prayer meetings. The only adverse remarks were made by some of the members of other

[176

Protestant churches because they were not privileged to skip two services a week.

As it was, many parents of high-school students said they would rather have a pastor like my father who kept their sons and daughters absorbed in athletics six days a week than have a pastor whose only interest was in preaching well-meaning but inconsequential Sunday sermons condemning the sinfulness of modern youth.

Having become accustomed to being criticized in the past for some of his dissenting opinions about certain Protestant religious practices, Ira Sylvester was not disturbed by unfavourable remarks about him as a high-school athletic coach. This would happen when bets had been made and the high-school football team lost an important game or when he and the school bus-driver took an overnight trip with a basketball team of ten or twelve otherwise unchaperoned teen-age girls.

One of the betting men in town, a dentist, had a mild complaint about Ira Sylvester, because once he had lost a hundred dollars on the final football game of the season.

That was the time I asked him how about the chances of winning that football game. That's all I asked and then he wanted to know why I was so anxious to find out something like that. I told him I was a big supporter of the high-school team and always yelled my head off at every game played.

He knew all about me and why I was trying to find out something. He wasn't easy to fool. That's why he looked straight at me and sort of smiled a little. You could count on him not preaching at you like a lot of preachers think they have to do.

What he did was start talking about how bad a shape the team was in. He said two of his best players had banged up knees from a game they played the week before and another one was still limping with a swelled-up ankle he got in another game and that the second-string substitutes didn't have enough weight to stand up against a big heavy team.

He talked like that for a long time, shaking his head and looking sadder every minute, and it made you think he wanted to call off the game so no more of his boys would get hurt. He even got me feeling sad about our boys getting run over like that by a lot of big boys.

By that time, nobody with any sense would've bet on that team without getting all the points in the world and even then I wouldn't feel easy about taking the risk on my hundred dollars, not after the way he talked.

Then you know what happened? He started talking about his two quarterbacks and how smart they were and how good they could throw passes. He looked real pleased while he was talking about them and you couldn't help thinking he was dead sure about winning that game.

Well, by the time he finished he'd got me so mixed up I was scared to take a chance betting either way on that game—win or lose, points or no points. And you know what? They won that game so easy scoring big with those three little boys playing sub-stitute that I even felt sorry for the big boys on the team they beat.

He stopped me on the street after the game and asked me how I'd liked it. He was trying to find out how I'd bet without coming straight out and asking. I told him the truth. I told him I'd got so mixed up about it beforehand from listening to him that I wasn't never going anywhere near him again to try to find out how he figured a certain game would go.

He looked real pleased to hear me say that, because he was glad to know I'd been too mixed up and scared to make a bet after listening to him. That's when he said he always tried to keep his team from getting over-confident, because that was a sure way to lose a game, and besides that it spoiled the game for football fans if they thought they knew for sure how it would end before it was played.

I never tried to find out anything from him in advance after that, which was the exact way he wanted it. He wasn't the kind to give inside tips for people to bet on his high-school boys. He wanted them to play football for their own good—not for people like me to bet on.

It was several years after Ira Sylvester's death when I asked one of his younger brothers if he knew their mother's reason for asking my father to study theology and enter the ministry instead of encouraging him to become a teacher or to go into some other profession after graduation from college.

My uncle said he was surprised that I would ask that question since he thought my father would have told me about it long ago. I said I had asked him and all he had said was that when he left home to enter college his mother had asked him to become a minister in the A.R.P. church. It had been left at that, and since he had not been inclined to talk about it further, I had neither asked him what his mother's particular reason was for making the request nor if he had made a promise of any kind to her. And then my uncle told me.

Bud's answer was as truthful as far as it went, and I suppose he thought it would be reaching too far back into the past to try to explain the circumstances about something that had happened that long ago. Anyway, Mamma had a reason for asking him to do that. And from her point of view it was a good reason.

And so when Bud didn't explain it more fully, I suppose he left it at that because he didn't want to say anything that might prejudice you in regard to religion. He had the idea that education without prejudice gave a person a better ability to get along in life. This was not because he believed a trained mind was an end in itself but that it provided the means for making intelligent

179]

decisions—and that the best decisions were those not influenced by prejudice.

That's probably why he never talked to you about whatever his own religious belief was or tried to impose it upon you. What he did was to expose you to life and religion. And if you didn't learn plenty going around the country with him, it's your own fault. He gave you the opportunity. You couldn't watch the celebration of mass and communion and the rites of foot-washing and smearing blood on the face without being glad to have the freedom to accept what you want of religion or to reject it entirely.

I'll tell you another thing about Bud. He wasn't any more interested in religion or concerned about it than I was—which means very little—when he finished high school and was ready to go away to college. But Mamma was, and that's when she told him that she wanted him to be a minister. I didn't hear what she said to him but, whatever it was, it was enough to get him to do it for her sake.

Mamma was a church-goer if you've ever seen or heard of one. She lived for it six days of the week and counted the days to Sunday. The only time I ever knew her to fail to go to church on Sunday was when she was too sick to get out of bed—and she never let that happen to her often in her lifetime. Don't ask me how she got that way, because I never knew. I suppose religion hit her hard, just like it does a lot of other people, and it stayed with her all her life. Anyway, she read her Bible every day and she prayed a lot and she did everything a devoutly religious person does.

But the trouble was that she could never get Papa to go to church or become interested in religion no matter how much she begged, pleaded, fussed, or scolded. Papa would do anything else she wanted, but not that.

There were a lot of times when Mamma tried to get Papa to read the Bible, but he'd say he didn't have the education to read the big words. When she brought the preacher to the house to pray, Papa would remember something he had to do in the barn-yard or out in the field. And if she tried to get him to go to church with her, he'd say he had to stay at home in case a mule got sick with colic and had to be doctored.

She was often provoked with Papa, and sometimes she cried, but she never lost her temper and became outright angry or called him an atheist or said he was going to hell or anything like that. When she tried to talk to him about religion, all he'd say was that he was going to wait to see if religion proved itself.

That's the way it was at home and Bud grew up with it just as all the other five of us did.

I never did know how Bud felt about religion or about being a minister, either. He heard many of the arguments Mamma and Papa had, but he never took sides and I suppose he was forming his own opinions about it.

All I know is that before he left home for college, he'd go to church sometimes with Mamma and sometimes he didn't. Any-way, there were too many of us for everybody to go to church on Sundays at the same time in one buggy even with Papa always staying at home. That's the way it was and I don't think Bud ever went to church more than once every month or two. And when he stayed at home and didn't go fishing or rabbit hunting with Papa and me or some of the others, he read books all Sunday long.

After Bud left home to go to college, I never saw enough of him again to find out what he thought about what Mamma wanted him to do. He was in college and theological seminary for about six years altogether and he worked somewhere in summer and went to war in Cuba for a while. After that he was always travelling and preaching somewhere from the Carolinas to Arkansas and Texas.

I think Mamma was satisfied once and for all when Bud became a minister, because she never said a word to any of the rest of us about doing the same thing. It might have been that she wanted him to become a minister because Papa wouldn't go to church, or else because he was the oldest and she hoped he'd be an example for the rest of us. However, it didn't inspire me or anybody else to follow his lead. And she must have been completely satisfied, too, because she never said another word to Papa after that about going to church or praying or Bible reading.

I never knew what Papa thought about Bud's going to a theological seminary and studying for the ministry, but I know he was proud of Bud for getting a college education. If Papa had made any comment at all about his being a minister, I'll bet it would've been to say that one preacher in the family was enough until religion had proved itself.

Sixteen

AS IS TO BE EXPECTED, there have been some important changes in the theological tenets and religious
practices of white Anglo-Saxon Protestants in the Deep
South during the decades between the 'twenties and the
'sixties.

In addition to startling proclamations by radical young
theologians that God Is Dead and the innovation of
theatrical Pulpits In The Round, perhaps the most
distinctly noticeable change in religious dogma and style
of worship in Southern Protestant churches has been the
result of the persistently widening breach between the
fanatical fundamentalist and the conservative modernist
believers in a Supreme Being.

The conflict between the fanatical and the conservative
factions has been aggravated and intensified over the
years by the extremes of poverty and wealth dividing the
population politically as well as socially and economically.

The poor and under-privileged are as easily aroused
emotionally by cajoling evangelists promising a better life
hereafter as they are by opportunistic politicians promising an affluent life here and now.

Church-going wealthy sophisticated white Southerners,
feeling socially and economically secure, disdain any
display of their emotions in public and fulfil their religious
obligations by attending church services for an hour on

Sunday morning to sing hymns and listen to the pastor's unoffending platitudes.

During the course of these recent years the religious practices of the fanatical and the conservative have come to differ to such an extent that there are only two common bonds remaining between them. One of these is the Bible, though even then each faction is committed to conflicting interpretations of the Bible's wordings. The other bond is the awareness by fanatical evangelist and conservative pastor alike of the racial prejudice of the white Southerner and knowing it is expedient to refrain from making an inflammatory reference to integration or civil rights. Only the exceptionable minister would fail to confine his remarks from the pulpit to praise of God and renunciation of sin.

The great majority of Protestants, however, are neither fanatics on the brink of lunacy nor ultra-conservatives on the verge of emotional calamity. These are the common, ordinary, neighbourly, everyday people living in lonely farmhouses, in small-town bungalows, and in crowded city apartments. They are the hundreds of thousands of church-going and tithe-paying citizens who have an unshakable allegiance to a particular faith or sect—the great masses of conscientious people to whom the earthly solace of religion and the prospect of heavenly immortality provides spiritual comfort and peace of mind.

Perhaps some of these thousands of religion-conscious people have been brain-washed and prevailed upon to become converts to a particular religious sect by high-pressure evangelism or by zealous relatives. Others may have joined a church merely to acquire prestige in social and business life in a religion-dominated community where a successful businessman's motto is Christ Was The First Rotarian or Don't Sell Christ Short. And some may attend church services and profess a religious belief only for fear that otherwise they will be lonely and forgotten and without friendship.

For the most part, though, church members in city, town, and country are those who have inherited a traditional religious belief from parents and grandparents. And just as those in a community who take excessive pride in an ancestral name, people with the status of having been born to a religious faith feel superior to latecomers who are merely converts.

But whether churchly by conversion or by heritage, many people would be as incapable of justifying their particular denominational membership as they would be if called upon to defend their reason for allegiance to the same political party of their forefathers. Nevertheless, these are devout Christians who accept without question the beliefs of a particular religious faith with the same inevitability that they glorify and assiduously perpetuate the ancestral name from generation to generation.

The white Southern Protestant, saint or sinner, clings to his religious convictions with unshakable tenacity. Whether he has performed acts of good will or acts of ill will during the past week, he rarely fails to be in his church pew on Sunday bowing his head with proper piety.

It is in this expansive and populous homeplace of the evangelized Southerner that are to be found the intelligent, educated, progressive, trustworthy, generous, and kind-hearted people of good will who personify the character of the community in which they live. The communities in which these forces predominate are not always easily found in a miasma of prejudice, but at least they do exist one after the other throughout the Deep South.

At the same time in every Southern community, large or small in population, there is usually either an active or potentially active underground organization of night-riding, intimidating, terroristic opponents of civil rights and social justice for non-whites, who on Sundays worship God in their churches by ostentatiously manifesting sighs and groans and hallelujahs of religious ardour. These are the die-hard segregationists, the feudal-minded, the hard-core white supremists, the inveterate Negro-haters who on week-days have no compunction about conveniently ignoring the Biblical precept that proclaims the brotherhood of all human beings. This division among Protestants in the Deep South and the formation of fanatical and conservative groups did not result from a religious dispute but was brought about by the revolutionary social and political progress of the 'sixties.

Earlier in the century, religion was aloof and apart from secular life and it existed for spiritual values alone. There was no compromise in that era with worldly affairs. On one hand, a man was dedicated whole-heartedly to a particular faith or sect and willingly became a volunteer layman who devoted more time and energy to churchly duties than to his business or profession. Otherwise, he was looked upon as being one of the lost souls who refused to be convinced that religion was more important than any accomplishment he could achieve in the outside world.

Later, however, it was realized it would be expedient to seek economic help outside the church in order to fulfil evangelistic ambitions. This was when Protestant denominations wanted large sums of money to build

[186

temples and tabernacles and missions in growing cities and to establish their denominational schools, seminaries, and colleges. And so the previously-scorned businessman was implored to bring money and come into the church on his own terms.

The resulting amalgamation of religion and business flourished in its time and accomplished its purpose. But, as in all eras in Protestant history, it came to an end with bitter quarrelling and recriminations. In this instance, the cause was not a doctrinal dispute but a secular disagreement about contemporary church policies concerning racial equality and civil rights. It was at this juncture, when no unity could be found, that the fanatics went in one direction and the conservatives happily took to the opposite direction. Even though each faction was glad to be rid of the other, neither one of them opened its church doors to non-whites.

Whatever the next era in Southern Protestantism will bring, it is evident in the 'sixties that the interwoven secular and religious fabric of civilization in the Deep South has become threadbare and outmoded with time.

Somewhat shamefaced and feeling ill at ease, enmeshed in the tattered web woven by well-meaning but socially-inept people of past eras, a new and more enlightened generation is already changing and trying to improve the texture of the fabric of the future.

In time to come there will probably be splits and up-heavals more drastic than any of those of the past, but at least now there is some assurance that Southern Protestantism, whether practised in bare-floor store-front missions or in plush-carpeted stain-glassed tabernacles, has the desire and the ability to survive for at least one more generation.

*At the Other
End of Town*

One

WHILE ANGLO-SAXON PROTESTANTS in the Deep
South were fervently evangelizing the people of their own
colour in town and country from border to border during
the early years of the twentieth century, Southern Negroes
were considered to be undesirable converts to Christianity.
Even though white Protestant missionaries were being
sent to Africa to save the souls of the heathen black natives,
at home it was feared that Southern Negroes might rebel
against staying in their assigned place if they became
imbued with too much of the spirit of Christian brotherhood and would presume to be privileged to fraternize
socially and politically as well as religiously.

This exclusion from the great white evangelical
campaigns in the Deep South left Negroes where they had
always been—on the outside. And, for their part, the
concern of Negroes at that time was not about the status
of their souls in life hereafter but about immediate
physical survival and well-being in a hostile social and
economic environment on earth. The prospect of the
salvation of their souls by a white Jesus Christ and a
continuation of outcast life in heaven administered by a
white God lacked the human appeal of better treatment in
earthly life.

Unlike Northern Negroes whose churches had been
established from Philadelphia to Boston long before the

Civil War, few Southern Negroes, no matter what their spiritual yearnings may have been, had the slightest knowledge of any organized religious faith when they were freed from slavery. In this primitive society, it was inevitable that the rumours of mysterious workings of God would be incorporated, along with a rabbit's foot and a cow's horn and rattlesnake buttons, in the superstitions of the people.

Even after slavery it was generations later before the ruling white society gradually permitted elementary schooling to liberate Southern Negroes from absolute illiteracy so they could read the wording of the Bible or anything else in print. In the meantime, and well into the twentieth century, the only knowledge Negroes had of organized religion was that which was exemplified by the Sunday church-going piousness of the white Protestants.

The few Southern Negroes who had been exposed to the churchly services of the Anglo-Saxon Protestants were former slaves. These were the elderly and subservient— Uncle Pete and Aunt Mariah and Mammy Beulah—who had been granted the distinction of being called good coloured people and thereby permitted to sit in the white-church balcony on Sunday. Even so, admittance to the balcony, which was called nigger heaven by the whites in the early plantation South, was more by command than by invitation.

The bestowal of this Sunday privilege helped to salve the conscience. As such, it was a kind of belated and final reward for a lifetime of proper obeisance while working for meagre food, clothing, and housing as yard boys, house maids, cooks, nurses, body servants, and other domestics. Plantation field hands and gang labourers— men and women—were looked upon as being too soil-

[192

encrusted and unwashed and uncouth to be granted this privilege.

For many years following the Civil War, though, after the death of the elderly domestic servants and when all Negroes had been banished from white-church balconies as an assertion of white supremacy and prescribed segregation, Negroes in the South working as field hands and sharecroppers were too impoverished to be able to build churches of their own.

Just the same, except for domestic servants, Sunday was a day of rest and, instead of church services, there were community gatherings of Negroes beside a creek in summer and around a log fire in a grove in winter. At these outdoor meeting places the principal activity other than the sharing of food and conversation was the singing and chanting of secular work-gang songs. Since there were no hymnbooks and no knowledge of sacred songs, as time went on many of these secular songs and chants of the fields were gradually changed in wording until in paraphrase they eventually become proper religious spirituals for singing in church.

However, regardless of the intent and wording of the spirituals, the original musical notes and tempo of the work-gang songs remained unchanged over the years. And, moreover, many of these spirituals long ago crossed the racial border and are, unknowingly and in all innocence, being sung now many years later in some Southern Protestant churches to the original tunes of the uninhibited erotic chants of work-gang Negroes when playing-the-dozens.

The implications expressed in playing-the-dozens were either in satiric and uncomplimentary references to the unadventurous sexual practices of the white race or the implications were in outspoken references to real and

193]

imaginary sexual adventures among men and women of their own race. When among themselves, the chants were unrestrained; when a white man could overhear, the chants were carefully veiled.

The unlimited scope of playing-the-dozens went far beyond references to sexual innovations of a white man and a Negro girl and even farther beyond the explicit description of a prolonged and tantalizing enticement of a Negro man by a white young missy. These are the erotic work-gang chants of Negroes in the cotton field and sawmill that became spirituals when they went to church and jazz when they went to town.

It was not until early in the twentieth century, fifty years or more after the Civil War, that it was economically possible for even a few Negro churches to be built in Deep South small towns and country communities. Even then, however, the Negro population continued to be over-whelmingly rural and illiterate and, without the ability to read, Bibles and hymnbooks were still useless even when available.

Religious services under these circumstances were primitive and for the most part were devoted to the singing of spirituals. Instead of a sermon and prayers, it was customary for somebody to be inspired to stand up and deliver an expanded and greatly enhanced version of a familiar Biblical story.

The most frequently retold story of all—which had been handed down from father or grandfather who had heard it in a white-church balcony during slavery—was that of Jonah and the whale. Elsewhere, only a few urban churches in that era had the possibility of having the leadership of a literate minister who could read passages directly from the Bible and recite the wording of hymnbooks.

When churches were built in agricultural regions—and very few Negroes lived elsewhere at the beginning of the nineteen-hundreds—for a long time the memberships were small compared with the population. The principal reason why many Negroes were reluctant to join a church was because they had no desire to be converted and become obligated to what appeared to be a segregated branch of white-race Christianity. Since Christianity as personified by the Anglo-Saxon Baptists and Methodists was the only religion known to them, and that was so definitely associated with the white boss and landlord, there was fear that they would be compelled to spend eternity where the white-race God would continue to force upon them the same cruelty and injustice they had always known.

As Negro churches were built, however, most of them had neither steeple nor belfry and the buildings remained purposely unpainted. Lack of money to buy paint and a church bell was not the only reason for this. Since it was customary for Anglo-Saxon Protestants to erect spires and paint their churches white, not many Negroes were inclined to attend religious services in a tall-steepled, gleaming white building that to them had become symbolic of white-race domination.

Later during this era of economic subjection in the agricultural South, particularly from the early nineteen-hundreds to the First World War, many Negroes came to realize that the only earthly place of temporary refuge from the torment of their lives was in a church of their own. And, more than that, unlike a creek-side or pine grove, a church building provided a roof for summer rains and a warm enclosure in winter for their community meeting place.

This was a realistic awakening, not a religious one, to the benefits a church building provided. And being immediate and here-on-earth, soon Negro communities across the Deep South began seeking ways and means to build churches no matter how small and unimposing they had to be. Just as playing-the-dozens in improvised lyrics had provided a means of making satiric comments about white boss and landlord, the church became a place of escape from white domination.

Since Negroes themselves could raise very little money, they willingly accepted help from white boss and landlord. Contributions for this purpose were considered to be a good investment by the white Protestants who believed, just as had their slave-owning forefathers, that a religious Negro would be a good Negro and not a troublesome one. By encouraging the Negro in this way to expose himself to the pacifying influence of religion while at the same time denying him even elementary schooling, it was anticipated that he would continue to be illiterate and subservient and fearful of making demands for better human treatment.

However, the eventuality was inclined to differ from the anticipated. As it usually happened, when a church was erected in a Negro community early in the present century, it was essentially a sanctuary for escape from the harsh and autocratic rule of the same people who had made the building of it possible. Just as the sole purpose of a plantation owner's cyclone cellar was for self-preservation, in those early years a Negro church was built to be a place of refuge in an oppressive social and economic climate.

Later, religious services in these churches were used primarily to express gratitude and to give thanks to the white man's God for being permitted to have the earthly sanctuary. And, so as not to risk offending a passing white boss and landlord and causing him to be suspicious of so much exuberance, gratitude was more safely expressed in vague wording of song and chant than in the explicit words of sermon and prayer.

Since the Southern white population was predominantly Baptist and Methodist, Southern Negroes found it expedient in the beginning for their churches to be identified as either Coloured Primitive Baptist or African Methodist Episcopal. This identification was pleasing to the ruling whites since it honoured the names of the two dominant Anglo-Saxon denominations and at the same time left no doubt that the Negro churches were racially apart from those of the Anglo-Saxon Protestants.

Actually, though, Negroes had no other choice under the circumstances. Other Southern fundamentalist sects, such as the Pentecostals and the Holiness, refused to permit religious affiliation with people of colour other than white and prohibited the use of their denominational names even for segregated Negro churches.

It was in these tolerated Negro Baptist and Methodist churches across the agricultural South that a few hours of weekly freedom from the demands and restrictions of white boss and landlord could be enthusiastically celebrated.

The celebration, except for an occasional impassioned retelling of a familiar Biblical story, consisted of almost continuous singing and chanting of improvised songs which were not always carefully worded in lyrics for a religious occasion—and frequently with spontaneous dancing in the aisles, too. These songs were accompanied by hand-clapping and foot-tapping since rarely were there any musical instruments available in small towns and rural communities.

These improvised spirituals, most of which still had the erotic implications and flavour of their secular work-gang origin, took the place of formal hymn singing where no hymnbooks existed. Impromptu prayers, which began as supplications and soon became lamentations, were loudly intoned with the same musical beat and tempo of the spirituals. All this was the folk music of the Southern Negro.

From this early beginning with a few scattered churches —and regardless of whether the motivation was secular or religious—it was well into the twentieth century before a majority of Southern Negroes had a gathering place of their own between walls and under roof. While being a church in name and a means of temporary escape from the white world, more than all it had become a community meeting hall where sorrow and pain and joy and elation could be expressed without restraint in spirited song and musical chant.

White Southerners, hearing the Sunday celebration of a Negro congregation, were not always able to resist the appeal of the songs and chants and soon incorporated them—without acknowledgment of origin—in their own culture.

In the present-day Deep South, it would not be unusual for a dedicated segregationist or racist to proclaim that only white people should be permitted to sing certain spirituals. One song in particular, 'When The Saints Go Marching In,' has been named as one that Negroes should not be permitted to sing and that it should be set aside for the exclusive use of the white race.

.　　.　　.　　.　　.

The elderly white storekeeper in a small town in the farming region of Southern Alabama did not hesitate to talk about Negroes and their way of life as he had known it. His small general merchandise store, an aging sun-and-rain-weathered wooden building with a sagging porch, was within a block of the Negro section of town and his customers were of both races.

It was a rainy afternoon in midsummer and the only person who had come into the store during the past quarter-hour was a small mulatto girl with an empty coke bottle. She had a nickel to spend for candy for herself and a dime to pay for another bottle of coke for her mother.

I sure do still remember some of the old-time darkeys—the hunched-over old uncles and aunties acting scared to death to stand up straight anywhere near spitting distance of a white man. And staying out of spitting distance had to be pretty far away from a mean-tempered tobacco-chewing landman boss. I've seen them when they could splatter tobacco juice on a rusty nail-head fifteen feet away—and in the white of a darkey's eye, too, with the same sure aim.

I always felt sorry for darkeys coming in here in my store all hunched-backed like that and I'd tell them they didn't have to stoop over and scrape on the floor around me. But they was so used to doing it around any white man that I reckon they just couldn't get themselves to do it any different at their age. I'm a white man and I believe in the races living apart. But they're people too, and I don't like to see them made to suffer just because they're not white like me.

Well, the old-time darkeys I'm talking about lived mostly down on the big plantation farms on the level land below here. That's where they was born to die. And they never knew nothing but hard work from sunup to sundown and no pay to speak of all their lives. I never saw a landman boss beat one of them, but

I've heard plenty about it all my life. I'm convinced that's why the old-time darkeys grew to be hunched over like that around a white man—growing hunched over showed the landman boss how slavish they was to him.

Anyhow, they lived mostly down there by the river in one-room sheds so tumbled down and roof-rotted you wouldn't want to keep a cow in and never had much to eat except corn meal and fat-back and turnip greens—but maybe some molasses, too. They couldn't grow much of a garden for themsleves, except some turnip greens, because the landman planted cotton and corn right up to all four sides of the sheds they lived in. But maybe two or three times a year the landman would let them have one of his pigs to butcher and hang up to smoke and cure.

The times when I used to see them most was when their landman hauled some of them to town in a team-wagon or truck to let them get treated by the doctor for some bad ailment—like a fester in the eyes or gangrene in sores—and maybe he gave them a quarter or half-dollar to spend for something they wanted to buy. Some of them was the raggedest people you ever saw, because that was the only clothes they had.

When they came in here in my store, the woman would want to spend her little money to buy a spool of thread and some buttons and things like that and maybe a little piece of cloth to sew and patch with if she had enough for that. The man always wanted to spend what money he had on snuff or smoking tobacco. But if he had a little left over he might buy his wife a little sack of candy, too. Those darkeys craved candy and tobacco just like anybody else. They was so natural about it like any human can be that it made me feel sorry for them getting treated the way the landman did to them.

After they'd left my store, sometimes I'd say to myself that I wished everybody was the same colour—any one colour—black or white or anything else—so nobody'd be born to be treated bad because of their colour. That's what I'd say to myself—you couldn't go around here for long saying that out loud where there's so many race-touchy white people who'd put you out of business or something else just as bad if they got mad at you.

I've been around the old-time darkeys a lot in my life and maybe I know them as good as any white man does. They never was anything like the new generation of their race—this new generation is all independent and getting educated and not too much scared to speak their minds about anything. I admire them for wanting their rights and it's all right with me as long as they don't come around and make trouble for me and so far they don't do nothing like that.

I know they're suspicious of all white people, but I'd say let those young ones keep on just like they're doing—and keep on minding their own business, too. I don't want them to turn against me and I'm not going to turn against them like some white people do for no real cause at all. I'd be in bad shape if they didn't come to my store to trade. A lot of them are making good money now and that's something the old-time darkeys never did.

The old-time darkeys I'm talking about grew up right here after the slave days, but they was hardly no better off than being slaves themselves. Being born free didn't help them enough to count much. They still didn't have hardly nothing—not even enough to live like ordinary poor people right here in town.

I know all about them living down there in those sheds and patching their rags to wear and eating that little corn meal and pig meat the landman gave them and maybe getting fifty cents when he hauled them to town two or three times a year. There wasn't much I could do for them when they came in my store except maybe give them a little extra measure of candy or tobacco when they spent a nickel or dime for that.

Whatever religion they had, it was their own special kind and not like any kind I ever heard about. I never did know how they got hold of the kind of religion they had, because there was no preachers down there to tell them anything—it just had to be something they worked up themselves. Anyhow, I favoured that, because I'd hate to see them make damn fools of themselves the way some white people will do who listen to their preachers—like the Snake Handlers and Holy Rollers and Hammer Heads and such.

I'll tell you the best I can about the kind of religion some of the old-time darkeys had—both the men and women. One time I remember was once when I went down there where a lot of them lived in their sheds. They had put together a little shack of a church at a crossroads. They called it a church, but nobody else could've seen how it could pass for that. It was just a plain slab-sided shack with an old piece of rusty tin roofing they'd found somewhere and it had two board-hinged windows and a makeshifty door. It looked more like a run-down old field-house where cotton pickers dump their cotton in if it starts to rain.

Well, on the inside they'd put together some wobbly wooden benches to sit on with no backs to them to lean against and they had a little tin stove with a stovepipe they stuck out one of the window openings when they built a fire in it in cold winter. And there wasn't another single thing in there—no pulpit or nothing. What they called a church was no bigger enough to hold more than twenty or thirty people even when they crowded close together like they had to.

It was a pretty warm Sunday night in the summertime when I was down there and I sat outside on a stump where I could look in the door and listen all the time. I tell you, it sure was something to see and hear.

I was there about a whole hour and all that time they didn't do a single thing like you'd expect in a church—no preaching or praying or nothing. And not much singing, neither—like they didn't have nothing worth singing about.

What those old darkeys did was moan and groan—and they done it like they was fixing to die right there. It sure was a pitiful sound to hear all of them doing that at the same time. Now and

[202

then they'd stop their wailing not for long and sing something like it was being made up all the time. But that never lasted long. And all the rest of the time it was moaning and groaning as loud as they could. Some of them got down on their knees when they done it—just like some people do to pray in a real church. But that was only the first part of it.

The other thing they started doing was to go to the walls and stand there beating on the pine slabs with their hands and fists and moaning and groaning at the same time like a landman was beating them to death. I couldn't figure out why they acted like that and I didn't find out till I asked one of the old darkeys to tell me why. Like all of them, he didn't want to say much about anything to a white man.

But I kept after him to tell me why everybody in there was wailing like they was going to die and he told me he didn't know exactly except it made him feel a lot better after he'd groaned as loud as he could and beat on the walls with his fists. I kept on some more asking him how it made him feel better and he said that little church was the only place where he and the rest of them could go and groan and wail away their misery and not make the land man mad.

The darkey said doing that helped to get rid of the misery better when everybody could do that at the same time together, but scared to do it anywhere else. The landman told them they could put up the little church out of scrap lumber for religion but couldn't have meetings in somebody's house where they might forget about religion and do too much talking about other things.

I asked him what the name of the church was and what kind of religion it had. He said it had no name at all and was just their kind of religion. I could believe that, because they had no preacher to preach and pray. And they didn't have to tell me that even if a preacher came along they couldn't never take up enough of a collection to pay him for it. Those poor people couldn't raise a dollar for that even if Jesus Christ had stopped by to preach to them.

Being a lukewarm Baptist myself, I didn't know whether to feel sorry or not for those darkeys about the kind of religion they had. But it looked to me like they got just as much good out of what they did with all their moaning and groaning and beating on the walls as most white people here in town got out of the Baptist or Methodist religion with a paid preacher and a fine church with a high steeple and pews with backs on them to lean back on and just sit there and do nothing. It makes you stop and think about what religion is good for if all you do is sit and listen to talk about it.

But all that was a long time ago now and times have changed. Most of those old-time darkeys are dead and gone and that shack of a church down there is all tumbled down. Most of the young generation of the coloured left those farms down the river a long time ago and came to town to live. They had to do that because the landman put in tractors and combines and didn't let many of them stay there no more.

This young generation of the coloured here in town have got two fine brick churches now and they hire preachers for both of them. Another big difference is that the coloured preachers can stand up and read the Bible out loud and everybody can read the words in the hymnbooks.

Maybe that's a good thing. But I don't know if their religion nowadays is any better for them than what the old-time darkeys had when all they did was that loud wailing and beating on those splintery pine-slab walls with their fists.

But the biggest change it looks to me like is that this young coloured generation is using their churches these days for all kind of things not like any kind of religion at all. They have meetings in them nearly every week about voting and integration and civil rights and such things. Maybe that's what churches for the coloured are best for now—a sort of up-to-date way of moaning and groaning and beating on the walls.

The way I hear the preacher at my church tell about it, there's only one heaven and that means there's no separate one for the blacks.

If that's true, then I don't see why the coloured would want to get so religious they'd want to go there. If they went there, they'd have to put up with the same things up there all over again that bothers them already down here. Anyhow, that's how I'd look at it if I was one of them.

Two

MOSES COFFEE FOR SEVERAL YEARS had been the Negro sexton of the Associate Reformed Presbyterian church in Bradley, South Carolina, where my father was the temporary pastor for several months in the early nineteen-hundreds. Bradley was a small town with a cotton gin, a bank, railroad station, and several grocery and merchandise stores. It was in the sand-clay farming country in the western part of the state not far from the Savannah River.

The grey-haired sixty-year-old Moses Coffee had bright tobacco-brown colouring and was habitually stoop-shouldered as if he had spent his life carrying a heavy load on his back. He was still muscular of body, however, and his thick hands remained rough with calluses after many years of plantation labour.

The first time Ira Sylvester told me to shake hands with Moses, and the last time as well, he quickly drew his hand away after barely touching me. He was not accustomed to shaking hands with a white person and his hand trembled so much that the calluses left a tingling sensation in my hand. It felt as if my palm and fingers had been scraped with an axe-sharpening rasp, and he muttered apologetically for the roughness of his calluses.

In addition to his job as sexton of the A.R.P. church, for which he was paid a few dollars monthly, Moses

207]

Coffee had been employed as part-time janitor at the Bradley post office for several years and he received a small salary for his work there. Also, but without pay, he was the volunteer caretaker of the Mt. Zion African Gospel church and cemetery.

On weekdays Moses wore his faded and patched bib-overalls, and on Sunday he was always dressed in the black wool coat and baggy grey pants that somebody had given him in payment for several days of yard work. He and his elderly wife, Rose, whose colouring of skin was similar to his, lived in a two-room log shanty on the Negro side of the railroad tracks where she did weekly washing and ironing for several of the white families of Bradley.

Before coming to town to live, Moses had worked on field-gangs and at sawmills between Bradley and the Savannah River nearly all his life since he was about eight or nine years old. He had never known exactly how old he was, but he thought that had been his approximate age when he was taken from his parents and put to work on a plantation with other child-age Negroes.

He said he had never been able to find his mother or father, or any brothers and sisters, after being taken away and locked up at night with the other children in a mule stable. All his sons and daughters had married and moved to other towns in the Carolinas. Occasionally, one of them would come to visit Moses and his wife and bring several grandchildren for them to see.

At the age of sixty, which at the time he judged to be his approximate age, Moses Coffee had a broad and friendly smile for everybody. However, when spoken to abruptly or unexpectedly by a white man, and particularly by a stranger in town, it was not unusual for him to begin trembling violently and stuttering. At such times, being unable to speak distinctly and make himself understood,

[208

he would bow his head lower than normally over his chest and stutter apologetically as he backed quickly away from the white person.

Somebody who had known Moses for many years told Ira Sylvester that the reason for his intense fear in the presence of white persons was because in his early life he had often been severely beaten by plantation overseers. There were still scars on his face and neck that looked like welts made by a trace chain.

Moses had said that once when he was a young man he ran away from the plantation and tried to get to the Savannah River to swim across it to the Georgia side. However, he was caught before he could get to the river and charged with the theft of a pocketknife which he said he had found on a road. He was quickly sentenced to two years at hard labour on the county chain gang. When released from the chain gang, an overseer was waiting to take him back to the plantation. He was kept there until he was too old to maintain the same pace at work as the younger Negroes.

As sexton of the Associate Reformed Presbyterian church in Bradley, and in addition to unlocking the doors and ringing the bell in the steeple half an hour before the eleven o'clock services on Sunday morning, Moses brushed down the cobwebs and swept the floor and dusted the pews every Saturday afternoon. Since he was unable to read, whenever he found a scrap of paper on the floor, he saved it to show to Ira Sylvester in case it was of some importance.

Once a month he washed the windows and climbed the ladder to the belfy to grease the bearings of the big brass bell. And when there was a wedding or funeral service in the church, he always got there early to open the doors and then came back afterwards to make sure that all the windows, as well as the doors, were securely locked so roving mischief-minded boys could not get into the building and damage the organ.

In summer, when the windows were opened on Sunday in order to let cooler air circulate inside the auditorium, Moses spent part of the time on Saturday afternoon with an oil-soaked rag on the end of a long pole firing the new wasp and mud-dabber nests that had been made under the eaves during the past week. He said as sexton it was his duty to see to it that nobody would be stung while attending Sunday services.

In winter, he came to the church before dawn on Sunday morning and started a fire. Then he would stay there and stoke the coal fire in the big iron-belly stove near the pulpit and choir loft until at least that part of the large building was comfortably warm.

Throughout the year, Moses always stayed at the church on Sunday morning until the services ended, since he was dressed for the occasion in his black coat and grey pants, and it was his custom to sit on a stool in the vestibule between the outer doors and the doors to the auditorium. While sitting behind the closed inner doors, he was out of sight of everybody in the church, but he could hear the sermon and listen to the music and singing.

Some of the members told Ira Sylvester they were sure they heard Moses singing sometimes along with the choir and that something ought to be done about it. Ira Sylvester told them that what they heard was probably an echo of the fine singing of the choir.

Several times during cold weather that winter Ira Sylvester had urged Moses to leave the unheated vestibule and to sit in a vacant pew at the rear of the auditorium during the services. Since it was a large wooden building with an unusually high ceiling and could not be adequately heated in extreme cold weather, the congregation always sat in the front part of the church in order to be close to the stove on a very cold day.

Moses had always declined to leave the unheated vestibule, or even to open the inner doors, saying that white people would not want him to sit down in the same room where they were and he was too afraid to do anything like that. Each time anything was said about his sitting in the rear of the church, his hands would shake violently and he would begin stuttering.

However, on one of the coldest Sundays of the winter, Ira Sylvester, finding that Moses had such a bad cold that he probably should have stayed at home in such weather, did succeed in persuading him for the first time to leave the unheated vestibule and sit in the last row of pews. It was near-zero weather that day with crusty frost on the ground and the windowpanes were coated with ice. The few church members who had come to the services that morning even kept on their overcoats while huddling close to the stove.

Moses was shivering when he cautiously tiptoed from the cold vestibule and sat down in the vacant pew at the back of the church. He was far away from anybody, since there were nine or ten unoccupied pews between him and the people near the stove.

Only a few moments after he had sat down, he coughed, and immediately after that some of the people began turning around time after time and glaring with angry stares at him sitting far away in the rear of the church. Moses slumped lower and lower in the pew until only his face could be seen.

Long before the conclusion of the services, coughing with a deep cold in his chest, Moses got up and tiptoed to the vestibule and closed the inner doors. After that he went into the broom closet and stayed there out of sight until the whole congregation had left the church and started home.

When Moses finally came out of the closet and saw Ira Sylvester waiting in the vestibule, he was still trembling. Then when he tried to say something, he began stuttering so much that he was unable to make himself understood. As soon as he could lock the front doors of the church with shaking hands, he bowed his head as deeply as he could against his chest and then put on his hat. Still stuttering apologetically, he turned around and walked as rapidly as he could towards the railroad tracks and home.

The next morning two of the church members came to see Ira Sylvester. The December weather was still cold and frosty.

The two men, one of whom was a storekeeper whose name was Mr. Foxhall and the other was a farmer whose name was Mr. Bonner, stood at the fireplace hearth and warmed themselves for a long time while talking about the unusual cold weather and the winter illness it was causing in their families. They were invited several times to sit down in the chairs in front of the fireplace, but they said they could not stay very long and would rather stand close to the fire.

Presently, with a stern frown and a solemn shaking of his head, Mr. Foxhall, who did almost all the talking while the two men were there, stated what their purpose was for coming to see my father. Mr. Foxhall was a large man about fifty years old with pale thin skin that flushed with a pink glow when he was excited.

What Mr. Foxhall began by saying was that many of

the church members were badly upset, and some of them very angry, because Moses Coffee had sat in a pew of the A.R.P. church during Sunday morning services.

He was soon talking in a loud voice, his pale skin flushed and glowing, while Mr. Bonner nodded emphatically in agreement with everything that was said. Next, he said another serious matter was that some of the members had demanded that Moses be ordered to stop singing along with the choir even when he was in the vestibule out of sight. Finally, he reminded Ira Sylvester that this was South Carolina and not North Carolina or Virginia or any other northerly state.

After that, Ira Sylvester was asked if he was going to agree never again to invite or permit Moses Coffee or any other Negro to sit in a pew of the church or to sing in the vestibule. When Ira Sylvester was not quick to reply, he was warned that many members who helped to support the church financially were so upset about what had happened that they had threatened to stop contributing and in that case there would not be enough money collected to pay the salary of a minister.

Ira Sylvester had listened patiently for nearly half an hour without interrupting or showing any signs of disagreement and protest. After a long interval of silence in the room, Mr. Foxhall, frowning impatiently, asked him what he intended to do about two such serious matters.

Instead of answering the question then, Ira Sylvester began talking calmly about a recent incident that had taken place in Bradley.

What had happened was that a gang of rock-throwing white boys one Sunday night had broken every window-pane of the Mt. Zion African Gospel church. As was customary in Bradley then, the Negro church held its Sunday services at night, since most of the members worked for white families and were required to cook and serve the midday Sunday dinner. And as usual the Mt. Zion church was filled with people that Sunday night when the rocks were thrown. Some of them were hit by the rocks and others were cut by slivers of glass.

Everybody in town knew who the boys were and that their parents were members of either the A.R.P. church or the Baptist and Methodist churches. Some of the boys had even boasted on the street about how easy it had been to break all the windows and get away without being caught.

Since none of the parents of the boys had offered to contribute anything to help buy the new glass, the members of the Mt. Zion church were still trying to raise enough money among themselves to replace the broken windows. Consequently, it was not possible to heat the windowless church during the winter months and there was little likelihood that services could be held in it again until warmer weather in spring.

When Ira Sylvester had finished talking about the glass-breaking incident at the Mt. Zion church, Mr. Foxhall immediately began shaking his head and said that was an entirely different matter and had nothing to do with the complaint that he had allowed Moses Coffee to sit in a pew of their church the day before.

That was when Ira Sylvester told the two men that the purpose of it was to explain why he was going to invite the entire congreation of the Negro church to hold their services in the A.R.P. church on Sunday nights unless enough money was raised that week to replace all the broken windowpanes.

Both men were evidently convinced that Ira Sylvester was serious about inviting the Negro congregation to hold services in their church, because they went to a

[214

corner of the room and conferred briefly in low tones of voice.

When they came back to the fireplace after a few minutes, nothing was said about the possibility of taking some action to keep the Negroes out of their church. Instead, the storekeeper said they would get busy at once and raise the money to replace the broken window glass. However, he still insisted that Ira Sylvester would have to agree not to let Moses Coffee sit in their white-church pews again on Sunday mornings.

Ira Sylvester told them that he was certain that Moses Coffee was so fully aware of the custom of the country that he would rather attend Sunday night services in his own Mt. Zion church where he would feel at ease than sit through services in their church under any circumstances. Then he said the only way to make that possible was not only to replace the broken windows but also for the A.R.P. congregation to buy a large portable oil heater for the vestibule of their church so the sexton would not have to sit in the same auditorium with white people in order to keep reasonably warm during one of the coldest South Carolina winters in recent years.

Within a few days, and before the end of the week, there were new windowpanes in the Mt. Zion church and a large portable oil heater was bought for the vestibule of the A.R.P. church.

Even though the oil heater was placed in the vestibule of the church as agreed, Moses Coffee neither saw it nor even knew it had been put there for his benefit.

Early the next Sunday morning, another cold December day, Moses's wife, Rose, sent a young Negro boy to tell my

215]

father that Moses was too ill with a bad cold to get out of bed and come to the church to start the fire in the big stove. Moses had given the boy the church keys and he offered to make the fire that morning.

That same afternoon my father went across the railroad tracks to the other side of town to find out if Moses needed a doctor and money for medicine.

Moses' wife came to the door, weeping and wailing, and said he had died of pneumonia that morning before the doctor got there to do anything that might have saved his life. Then she said the funeral services would be held the next afternoon at the Mt. Zion church and Moses was to be buried in the adjoining cemetery where he had been the volunteer caretaker for many years. The Negro undertaker was already there and Rose had laid out Moses' black wool coat and grey pants for his burial.

Ira Sylvester said he gave Rose the money he had intended to leave to pay for medicine for Moses and then what was left in his pocket, too.

The following day Ira Sylvester was the only white person at the funeral service. He said that when the Negro minister asked him to say a few words at the graveside, he felt ashamed of himself for waiting until Moses Coffee was dead before expressing appreciation of him as a human being and apologizing for the hostile attitude of some of the church members when he left the unheated vestibule, with a cold that had developed into pneumonia, and came into the auditorium for warmth.

It was very cold and a drizzly rain was turning into sleet when he left the cemetery after the funeral and crossed the railroad tracks to the other side of town. He said he was walking along the main street and hurrying home when he was stopped in front of the general merchandise store owned by the man who had complained so angrily the

[216

week before because he had permitted Moses Coffee to sit in a pew of the A.R.P. church.

They went inside the store, which was warmed by a big coal stove, and Mr. Foxhall began talking about how foolish it was for a white man to go out in that kind of weather to attend the funeral of a Negro and run the risk of getting pneumonia himself. He said that just because Moses had been the A.R.P. sexton would be no reason to go to his funeral even in fair weather.

Then presently, in a sharper tone of voice, he said what was really disturbing him was the fact that the pastor of his church would go to the funeral of any Negro. As he expressed it, niggers made good store customers, but, after selling them some merchandise, he was not going to treat them like ordinary white people and neither should the pastor of his church. During all that time, Ira Sylvester listened attentively, occasionally shaking his head un-approvingly, and made no apology for what he had done.

After a while, Mr. Foxhall, seeing that Ira Sylvester still had not approved of his attitude, said that he did not want to be misjudged. He said he wanted it known that he was a good Christian, a good A.R.P., and a kind-hearted man. He talked earnestly for a while about his love for his wife and children and how he always did everything he could to help relatives when they were sick or had money troubles.

But after that, quickly reverting to anger with a pink glow coming to his pale face, he said he was a true and loyal white man and therefore was glad that Moses Coffee was dead so the trouble about his sitting in the same church with white people was in the past and could never happen again. He said Moses would never have dared to sit in the A.R.P. pew if he had not been hired as part-time janitor at the post office because working for the federal government made him think he was as good as a white man.

Ira Sylvester tried to protest against the way he was talking about Moses, but Mr. Foxhall, raising his voice louder, said nobody could keep him from saying what he thought about Negroes. Then he stated that he was going to see to it personally that the next Negro sexton hired for the church was going to have the fear of God and the whole white race put into him at the start so he would never dare sit down in the same place where there were white people.

Telling Mr. Foxhall that he had heard enough of that kind of talk and was not going to listen to any more of it, Ira Sylvester left the stove and walked through one of the aisles where various kinds of merchandise were on display. The counters and shelves were stacked, just like they were in the other two general merchandise stores in town, with family clothing and hardware and staple groceries. In one corner of the store there was a section where shoes were displayed and several chairs had been placed under a large notice stating that they were for the use of white customers only.

Smiling and his face no longer flushed with anger, Mr. Foxhall pointed at the white-only sign and said it was a good opportunity to prove that he practised what he preached. He took Ira Sylvester to a door that opened into a narrow shed that had been built for the use of Negro customers who would not buy shoes unless they could be tried on first.

There was a single wooden bench in the windowless shed and on one of the walls there was a bracket that held a thick, black, braided-leather whip which was about nine or ten feet in length and the kind that had been used for many years to drive ox teams at logging camps.

[218

Taking down the whip, Mr. Foxhall carried it into the store from the shed. He whirled the heavy black whip over his head several times and then slammed it against the floor with a jarring crash of leather and wood. As he stood there jerking the whip forwards and backwards, making a sound like a firecracker each time the strand snapped at the end, he said that was how he could put the fear of God and the whole white race into any living Negro and all of them yet to be born.

That was when Ira Sylvester, turning away and walking toward the street, told the storekeeper that evidently he had failed to accomplish enough good as a minister during the short time he had been in Bradley. He said he was going to consider staying a while longer instead of leaving in a few weeks, as he had planned to do, to become pastor of another church.

Walking beside Ira Sylvester and patting him friendlily on the arm, Mr. Foxhall begged him not to change his plans about leaving. Then picking up a large paper bag, he hastily filled it with candy and cigars and followed Ira Sylvester to the street. Still urging him not to let anything change his mind about leaving, the storekeeper thrust the big bag at him and insisted that he take the candy and cigars.

As my father was walking up the street, Mr. Foxhall called after him and told him that if he wanted anything else at all before leaving town, just to come back to the store as often as he felt like it and help himself to as much as he pleased.

Three

IN THE SMALL EAST GEORGIA TOWN where my
father was the pastor of the Associate Reformed Presbyterian church for a time shortly after the First World
War, it appeared to be that everybody was prosperous
and had an unlimited amount of money to spend—
everybody, that is, except the Negroes. And as it was, the
population of the town was about equally divided between
white people and Negroes.

One evidence of prosperity among the white citizens
was that farmers began moving to town and building large
houses with imposing porticoes. Another evidence was
that merchants stocked their stores with over-stuffed
furniture and the latest styles of clothing for women.

And in addition to all this, one of the two doctors in
town closed his office and devoted all his time to displaying
and selling expensive new automobiles of various makes
to the prosperous farmers and merchants.

There had been such a demand for the latest models of
automobiles when the doctor's display room was opened
that he soon opened a larger branch on the opposite side
of the street. When a buyer said he wanted to drive away
immediately in a new automobile and was not prepared to
write a cheque for the full cash payment, he was usually
accommodated.

That was when the doctor would offer to take a six-month mortgage on good farm land or valuable real estate in town with the provision written into the contract that the mortage would be foreclosed if it were not paid in full by the date of maturity. The doctor was so successful selling expensive cars and foreclosing real estate mortgages that he never reopened his office and practised medicine again. It was not long until he was able to move to Florida and retire.

During this inflationary era of several years that preceded the depression of the nineteen-thirties, the poverty and want of the Negro community, which was already conspicuously extreme, became increasingly severe.

The principal reason for this disparity was because, being landless and having nothing to sell at inflated prices, Negroes did not share in the wealth derived from the sale of farm and forest products, such as cotton and lumber, but during that time they had to pay excessive high prices for food, clothing, and housing. There were so many Negroes seeking work of any kind, and some of them were in such need, that when jobs were available, they had to accept by necessity whatever pay was offered. Consequently, wages became progressively lower and lower month by month.

The part of town where we lived was not far from the segregated Negro community and it was where many of them—men, women, and children from about seven years old and upwards—stopped first to offer to do any kind of work for whatever pay they would receive. The stronger men and women were paid as much as fifty cents for a morning's work and children usually received a dime.

Of the many Negroes who asked Ira Sylvester for a job of any kind, if only for a few hours with any pay he would receive, one was Rumson Tatum.

Rumson Tatum called himself a fellowship minister—

[222

not a preacher—and disclaimed relationship with any religion or church other than his own. He conducted his own particular type of services on Sunday nights in a small, unpainted, plank-sided building situated at the edge of the Negro section and within two short blocks of the first houses of the white residential part of town. It had taken Rumson about two years to collect pieces of donated scrap lumber and build the church with his own hands.

He was a tall, pleasant mannered, brown-coloured man about forty years old with a sturdy wooden leg which he had whittled from a hickory limb and which was strapped with leather belting to his right knee. He had lost the lower part of his leg in a band saw accident at a lumber mill when he was about thirty years old. Because of the handicap, he had not been able to get a steady job since the accident. And for one reason or another he was not married, but he lived with a young girl who was a part-time maid for a white family and kept house for him.

When Rumson held his services at the True Life Fellowship church, which was usually filled to standing room with a hundred or more people on Sunday nights, it was the one time when he lowered his trouser over the hickory peg. During the other days of the week he kept that trouser leg rolled above the knee so it would not be in the way while he was working at whatever job he could get.

That morning in midsummer when Rumson Tatum stopped and asked if he could do any kind of work, Ira Sylvester told him there were a lot of weeds in the garden that needed to be chopped down and that he could work for two or three hours at that job.

When the work was finished and he had been paid for it, Rumson came into the rear yard for a drink of water and then sat down on a bench in the shade.

While he was cleaning the mud from the lower part of his wooden leg, where mud had stuck to it when he was chopping weeds in the damp part of the garden, he told my father that a white man whose house was about two blocks from the True Life Fellowship church had complained to the chief of police that he was being kept awake on Sunday nights by loud music and singing. The chief of police had warned Rumson that if he received another complaint like that he was going to padlock the church and never let it be used again.

Rumson said he was worried about the complaint and was afraid the police would close the church. He said he had no resentment about the white people in town getting rich and having fine cars and big houses and he thought they ought to let him keep his church going so he could get a few dollars a month in the collection basket.

As he explained it, he was afraid people would find another place where they could sing and stop going to the True Life Fellowship church if they could not sing like they wanted to there. And he said as soon as the music started there was no way to keep them from singing without so much loudness. And more than, to provide the kind of music the people wanted, one of the members always brought his drum to church and beat a loud accompaniment to the organ music. It was a large bass drum that could be heard all over that part of town for several hours on Sunday nights and it did sound more like dance hall music than church music.

He said the reason people came to his church was because they were dissatisfied with the kind of religious services that were held in the other Negro churches where too much time was taken up with long sermons and prayers and not enough time devoted to music and singing. And what he did in the True Life Fellowship

[224

church was to say just a few words about religion and get that over with in a hurry so there would be plenty of time left for hymns and spirituals and anything else the people wanted to sing.

Rumson said he had built his church for fellowship, just like the name of it sounded, not for preaching, and that people who wanted the preaching kind of religion and liked to hear a lot of talking and praying about it could go to the Negro Baptist and Methodist churches. But his members wanted fellowship without being preached at about religion and that was why he had built the church just for them and called himself Fellow Rumson Tatum and not Reverend Rumson Tatum.

Ira Sylvester told him that it would be a violation of a town ordinance to disturb the peace, although at the same time he would not like to see the church closed and padlocked by the police. He suggested that the Sunday night services be temporarily suspended to the end of summer, which was only a few weeks away, and then when the weather turned cooler the door and all the wooden-shutter windows could be shut to keep the sound confined to the inside of the building and not loud enough to disturb anybody a block or two away.

After thinking about the suggestion for a while, Rumson shook his head. He said his members had to have a place to sing every week and he was afraid they might find another place to sing if he failed to let them into his church even one time. Instead, he said he was going to shut the door and windows the following Sunday night and have music and singing as usual no matter how hot the weather was.

As he got up to leave, Rumson thanked Ira Sylvester for the suggestion that would make it possible to keep the sound from disturbing anybody enough to make another complaint to the police. Then, pleased and smiling, he invited my father to come to the Full Life Fellowship church the next Sunday night and stand outside to hear how subdued the sound of music and singing would be.

There had been a violent though brief thunderstorm late Sunday afternoon that had cooled the air for a while. However, at twilight between eight and nine o'clock the August night was warmer and the air was more humid than it had been before the rain. Even after sundown in August, it was not unusual for the temperature to be in the eighties and nineties.

Ira Sylvester and I walked down the street in the late twilight toward Rumson Tatum's church. As was still customary then in many small towns in the Deep South, there were no Sunday night services at the Associate Reformed Presbyterian church and my father and I often went to some other church in town or in the country to watch the religious activities and rituals of various denominations.

When we got to the Negro section of town where there were no street lights, the night was completely dark except for a few faint stars. And when we got to the church, all we could see there were some streaks of pale yellowish light coming through narrow cracks in the wooden shutters.

The door of the building, like the shutters, was closed tightly and the music and singing sounded muffled and far away. Several times before when we had gone to a Negro church, we sat on the last rear bench or pew. This time Ira Sylvester said he wanted to stay outside to find out how much sound could be heard with the door and windows closed.

[226

We had been standing there for nearly half an hour when one of the wooden shutters was suddenly thrown open on its hinges and several people crowded at the open window and leaned out as far as they could to breathe the cooler air. At the same instant that the window had been opened, there was a blast of musical sound from inside the church that probably was heard many blocks away. And above all there was the loud throbbing beat of the big bass drum.

It was several minutes before Rumson Tatum was able to pull and shove all the people away from the window and close the wooden shutter. As soon as that was done, the sound of the drum and the singing was only faintly heard again.

On the way home later, and several blocks from the church, there was another loud blast of music and singing, with the beating of the drum above all, and there was no doubt that some of the people had again opened one of the windows to get some fresh air. Hearing the sound at that distance, and so late at night, it seemed certain that the man who had complained to the police the week before would be awakened by the sound and would probably do something about it.

It was not long after midnight when the wailing alarm at the downtown fire station was turned on and in a few minutes the fire truck came roaring up the street toward the Negro section with the shrill siren waking up everybody along the way.

When my father and I got to the street, we could see a red glow in the sky over the Negro section. And as we ran towards the fire, along with a lot of other people, a long streak of flame and smoke shot upwards from the burning building. When we got within a block of the flames, we could see that Rumson Tatum's Full Life Fellowship church was on fire.

227]

The firemen did not have enough water available in that part of town even to try to put out the fire and they were using the little water they could pump from a well to wet down the roofing of nearby dwellings to keep sparks from setting them on fire.

The roof over the rear part of the church was in flames, although the fire had not reached the front part of the church when Rumson got there. Hobbling on his wooden leg, he had not been able to get there any quicker. When he saw that the fire was still in the rear of the building, he said he had to save the organ and he hobbled to the front door. Somebody told him that the organ was in the part of the church that was already burning, but he ignored the warning.

While people were shouting to Rumson to come away from the building, he opened the door. A wall of flame and smoke burst through the opening and he stumbled and fell on the steps. Several men, shielding their faces with their arms, got to him in time and dragged him away.

Rumson's hair was singed close to his skull, there were burned holes in his shirt and pants, and the lower part of his wooden leg was charred and smoking. Two women who were members of his church, both of them wailing loudly, hurried to him and fanned his face with their skirts.

While Rumson sat on the ground rubbing damp dirt over the wooden peg to keep it from burning any more, he said that as soon as he could whittle a new wooden leg he was going to start collecting pieces of lumber to build another church so people would have a place to sing.

When the rafters crashed in flames and the walls collapsed, Rumson wiped the tears from his face. With a confident smile, he said the new Full Life Fellowship church would have plenty of electric fans all over it to keep people cool on the inside in summer and would be

[228

built without windows so it would be so quiet on the outside that nobody would bother to set it on fire and burn it down.

In the early nineteen-sixties, more than forty years after the burning of the first Full Life Fellowship church and the construction of the new and larger building, Rumson Tatum was still alive and making the same scanty living in his old age as he had done in the past. Although he was still unmarried, too, another young woman was living with him and keeping house for him.

Rumson was white haired and in his eighties then and he had attached a rubber pad to the lower end of his wooden leg so there would be less danger of his slipping on paved sidewalks and injuring himself.

Once a week as always, people living in the Negro part of town came to Rumson's church on Sunday for several hours to play musical instruments and sing. However, one difference now was that the concerts took place in the afternoon, and not at night, and there had been no complaints that the sounds disturbed the peace. Even people living across the street from the windowless building said it was so soundproof that they rarely heard music and singing.

Another difference in the nineteen-sixties was that the people who went to the church were much younger than had been the members forty years earlier and instead of playing an organ and bass drum they brought electrically-amplified guitars, accordions, trombones, trumpets, small drums, and other wind and string instruments to play rock-roll and modern jazz.

There was still some exuberant singing of hymns and

spirituals and folk songs. However, with so much interest among the young people in jazz and instrumental music and with everybody wanting to perform with his favourite instrument, much less time was devoted to song than to music.

Rumson Tatum said he had no objection to the change that had taken place in recent years. In fact, he was even pleased about it, because the larger number of people coming to the church than ever before created more fellowship.

Other than opening the Full Life Fellowship church on Sunday afternoon instead of at night, another change was that now Rumson collected a small door charge in advance instead of passing the collection basket later with uncertain and not always satisfactory results.

All had gone well at Rumson's church for a number of years until a group of young Negroes rented it for a Sunday morning meeting. They had paid Rumson the rent in advance and promised to vacate the building no later than noon so that his regular Sunday afternoon concert would be held as usual. Assuming they were going to use it for a special musical practice session, he had not asked what their purpose was for renting it.

A large crowd gathered at the church early that Sunday morning and several excited speeches were made about the newly-decreed policy of the white owner of a small café located next door to a truck-stop gasoline filling station.

What had happened was that a few days earlier the owner of the café, which was a one-man operation and not much more than a hot dog and hamburger stand, had placed a large sign at the entrance stating that only white persons would be served and that any other person entering the café would be prosecuted. When one young Negro stood in the doorway and said he wanted a

[230

hamburger-and-piccalilli to carry out, the owner called the police and had him arrested.

Many Negroes had jobs at filling stations along the busy street, and, since the particular café was the only one within several blocks, they had been in the habit of going there at various times of the day for hot dogs and hamburgers and carrying them out to eat elsewhere without attempting to sit at the counter. Several of the Negroes who had gone farther away to get something to eat at mealtime had had some of their wages withheld for having been away from the job too long.

When the owner of the café, a gruff-mannered man of middle age who for a while had been a deputy sheriff, was asked why he had decided to stop selling anything to Negroes, he said most of his white customers were truck drivers from all parts of the South and they objected to Negroes coming into the café while they were eating at the counter. And the more he talked about it, the more angry he became.

Finally, he said he had an even better reason for barring Negroes than just pleasing his white customers. As he explained it, he had been thinking for a long time about barring them because more and more of them were acting like they believed they had as much right to come into his café as white people and then talk to him as if they were as good as he was. He said that was why he had made up his mind that he was not going to listen another time to black people telling him how they wanted their hamburgers cooked and how much mustard and catsup or piccalilli for him to put on them.

At the meeting that Sunday morning in the Full Life Fellowship church, a few of the people said they wanted to break every window of the café and wreck the place. Some of the others were in favour of a sit-down demonstra-

231]

tion inside the café and said they were willing to be arrested. Instead, after nearly two hours of argument and discussion, the majority voted to picket the café with protest placards until the owner relented and let them buy from him again.

A committee was appointed to plan the picketing so that nobody with a steady job would have to take time off from work and lose pay but who would picket before or after regular working hours. It was decided that at least two persons who could arrange suitable hours would be walking up and down in front of the café with protest signs from the time it opened in the morning until it closed at night. A schedule was to be drawn up for a week of picketing to begin when the café opened Monday morning.

There were two pickets on the sidewalk in front of the café when the owner got there Monday morning at seven o'clock. Without a word spoken, he unlocked the door, and then in a few minutes he came back to the street with a heavy wooden pole and tried to beat them with it.

Angry and threatening when he found out that the two men were agile and able to avoid the blows, he said he was going to find out the names of the Negroes who were responsible for organizing the picketing as well as the exact location of the place where they had met to make plans for it. Then he warned them that somebody was going to be sorry because he was going to find out what he wanted to know and then do something about it.

Late that same night, after the café had closed and the pickets had left, Rumson Tatum's Full Life Fellowship church was burned down for the second and last time.

The next day the chief of police advised some of the Negroes to discontinue their protest at the café. He said he had heard that there would be more fires in the Negro section as long as the picketing continued.

[232

Four

FOR MANY GENERATIONS in the states of the Deep South, the white Protestants of the fundamentalist sects ranging from the élite Baptists to the menial Hammer Heads, while holding steadfastly to their individual religious ideologies, were in full accord in matters political. In sum, this meant voting the straight Democratic ticket and thereby opposing social and economic recognition of non-whites.

This united front enabled the fundamentalists to use a supreme political power to dominate and rule by effectively resisting the passage of progressive legislation that would have benefited and given encouragement to people of the Negro race.

The church vote, as it was called, and which was sufficiently powerful to rule the Democratic party in the Deep South, and even without the cooperation of the Catholics and Episcopalians, was able to depose and send into political exile any politician or statesman who ignored the dictates of the fundamentalists. To take the place of an exiled legislator, the demagogue was elevated to the position of leadership.

It was during this era that reactionary fundamentalist religion and states rights politics were amalgamated to such a degree that even in the nineteen-sixties they were still synonymous and inseparable.

Now after many decades the forces of opposition are gradually losing their power of domination and absolute rule over the Negro. In the course of national events, and by depletion by death, the older generation of fundamentalists is being supplanted by a more enlightened younger generation and the separation of church and state is already evident throughout the Deep South.

Even though there is sporadic resistance to legislation for the educational and social benefit of Negroes—locally and statewide in Alabama and Mississippi in particular—the progressive factors already predominate. For one thing, federal laws have been imposed and enforced. And perhaps most important of all, the young college-educated generation of Negroes is outspoken, confident, and vote-conscious about the rights and privileges of American citizenship. Wherever individuals and groups of this new generation have had responsible Democratic or Republican leadership, the power of the vote has already achieved more for them than strong-arm violence.

In colleges from the Carolinas to Louisiana, the new Negro of the Deep South is perhaps as politically aggressive and demonstrative as his white counterpart in universities from California to Massachusetts. After that, however, much of the similarity fades away. The most noticeable difference between them is that the white student is likely to shift his allegiance from one idealistic, or fashionable, cause to another while the Negro student is inclined to remain constant to his realistic and dedicated cause to surmout racial prejudice and attain democratic equality.

The goal of most Negro college students in the nineteen-sixties is not necessarily enrollment in a traditionally white university merely to achieve symbolic or token integration. Ordinarily, those who do want to enroll in such an institution are impelled by a different purpose. They are usually the ambitious and qualified students seeking higher and specialized education in graduate schools, which is not always available at Negro colleges, and which is necessary if they are to have careers in law, medicine, science, and professorships.

Otherwise, the larger number of Negro students in the Deep South will say they prefer to attend Negro colleges for basic education rather than face the social ordeal of being of the racial minority at the larger state and private integrated universities.

However, among the exceptions are many robust, six-foot-six, two-hundred-forty-pound football players at Negro junior colleges. These are the students who are scouted by midwest and far-west football coaches and offered such attractive athletic scholarships that every year an increasing number enroll in state and private universities all the way to the Pacific coast.

The twenty-year-old student, who, like his brothers and sisters, had the distinctive colouring and profile of a quadroon, was at home in Mississippi for his summer vacation. He had a two-month muscle-job, as he called it, working for a construction company building overpasses for a new highway. Before that he had graduated from his home town high school and then had attended a nearby Negro junior college for a year where he was a tackle on the football team.

Now he had completed a year's study, and received passing grades, at a large western state university where he was a lineman on the football team. His athletic scholarship at the university would pay all his expenses for two more years until graduation.

When I went out there a year ago, I took one look around me and I thought I'd got to the other end of the world. I'd never been much outside of Mississippi before except up to Memphis and over in Alabama and I didn't know what to expect when I left here. But I sure didn't think it'd be anything like it was out there.

I guess I was thinking it was going to be about the same kind of flat-dirt country like it is around here where the tall trees keep you from seeing very far at a time. But it wasn't. It was real different. It was sort of round-hilly everywhere you looked and a lot of big smooth brown rocks showing and no trees anywhere except the scrubby kind growing close to the ground more like blackberry bushes. The university was spread over the top of one of the hills and you could stand there and see dozens and dozens of miles away and that country still looked the same everywhere— sort of round and level at the same time. If I'd wanted to be, I could've been real homesick, but I didn't want to be.

Another thing was that it turned cold real fast just after I got there and it stayed that way nearly all the time. Anyhow, it felt cold to a Mississippi coloured boy like me. But I got used to it after a while and I sort of like it that way now. Besides, it sure puts a hustle in you when you're playing football, and practising, too.

That's a real pretty part of the country—all grassy green part of the time and then snowy white in winter. I sure am lucky about that.

The way I got out there so far from home was because I wanted to play big-time football and that was my big lucky chance. If I'd stayed here, I could've played one more year at the junior college. And then after that I knew I'd be up against it, because none of the big university teams in this part of the country ever sent somebody around to talk about it. These here don't come around that I know of looking for coloured boys to play on their teams. They play only white boys on their teams.

My big ambition is to play professional—on a big team in the National Football League or the American Football League—and I figured I'd never make it staying here and playing on a junior college team for a couple of years. Those big coaches in the pro football leagues wouldn't bother much about somebody like me playing only a couple of years at a Negro junior college down here in Mississippi and never playing real big-time college football like they do at Ole Miss and Georgia Tech and Alabama.

Man, I tell you, it sure made me feel good when the coach came down here from out west just to see me and said he'd heard all about me and had a lot of information somebody had sent him. When he told me all my expenses would be paid by a scholarship—tuition and room and board and all—besides a part-time job so I could make some spending money—he didn't have to say another thing. Man, I was jumping with joy. All I could say that it was the best thing that'd ever happened to me in all my life and I promised I'd be the first man there to start football practise.

We had a real good season last year—won eight and lost only two—in that tough conference—and it's going to be better next time. It looks so good I wouldn't be surprised if we won the conference title this time. And believe me, that's a knock'em-rock'em conference to play in. Most of the teams have one or two coloured boys just as hefty as me. And the white boys have got plenty of heft, too.

What I'm hoping for is that some people from the pro teams will be coming around this fall and talking about signing up to be a red-shirt. If I can get to be one of the lucky ones, I'd still have one more year on the university team to sharpen up for the pro big-time. I might not have a chance to pick and choose, but that won't matter. Just so one of them wants me, that's what counts. If I could pick and choose, though, I'd sure like to play for the

237]

Chicago Bears or the Cleveland Browns. I've never seen them play except on television, and both of them are great.

If I can make the grade in pro football and get a good start, I ought to be good for ten or twelve years. I figure that if I can get up there in a couple of years from now when I'll be twenty-two, I ought to be able to stay there till I'm maybe thirty-five. Then what I'd want to do is get a coaching job at some Negro junior college here in Mississippi or anywhere else. Putting all that together, that'd make my life for me. Maybe some day the big universities down here in the South will hire Negro coaches if they're good enough, but right now I'm not counting on it.

Right now my big job is to keep my grades up so I can stay on the team out there for the next two years. I can find plenty of time for study. That's no trouble. But getting good grades is the big thing.

I don't get much involved in the social life. Being my colour, you don't mix much—like going to dances and parties and things. I'm still a Mississippi coloured boy and I can't get over that even out there in the west.

It's the same about going to church out there. There're no all-Negro churches and I just couldn't forget who I am and go to a church full of white people. Maybe they wouldn't mind it, but I wouldn't feel right. I'd be shaking all over like I'd do if I put my foot inside a white church on Sunday in Mississippi.

I sit around sometimes and drink cokes or coffee with white girls in the student union, but so far that's all. Some of them like to tease me about not trying to make a date. Maybe they're serious, maybe not. Anyhow, I get all shaky like I would right here in Mississippi if a white girl said the same thing and can't think of much to say except something real silly or stupid. I don't know. Maybe by next year I might get up enough nerve for that. But standing here right now in Mississippi—I'm even scared to think about it.

Well, that's the way it is about the white girls out there.

[238

They're real friendly teasing me like that. But it's different with the white boys. I'm not saying they make a big thing of being white and treating me black. That's not exactly it. It's still a lot different out there than here in Mississippi—they don't act mean to me about anything. It's hard to say what the difference is. Maybe it's more like not belonging to the club or something. There're only four of us in the whole university and the white boys treat all of us alike. My roommate is another junior college transfer from Alabama with a football scholarship like I've got and he feels the same way I do about being on the inside and outside at the same time.

All I know is I'm not going to push myself at the white boys out there. I'm going to take it just like it comes. That's the best way. Sure, I get a lot of back-slapping and glad-handing and things like that during the football season. I don't mind that a bit. But after the last game, things just sort of drift away and you feel like you want to keep to yourself most of the time.

What I'm doing is learning how to live with myself as a Negro and not being ashamed of my colour when I'm around white people. If I'd stayed here in Mississippi all my life and not gone out there, I never would've learned anything like that to help me. If you're down here all your life, you'd never have a chance to learn much about white people, either. Here they put a big line right down the middle of everything and they stay on one side of the line and you stay on the other.

Man, when I get my full education, I'm going to be so proud of it that no white man is going to be able to hurt me with his talk and make me feel like the nigger some of them here want me to put up the show of being. That's what my education is for— knowing I'll have something in my head just as good as what some white people have and better than a lot of the others.

Of all the Negro communities in the Deep South, Atlanta has the largest educational complex and the largest number of churches. And within sight of a grade school, high school, college, or university, it is almost a certainty that there will be the spire of a church and, in all probability, a Baptist church at that. And, as in the white community, social status is regulated and ranked according to the location and affluence of the particular Baptist church of which a person is a member.

The Negro college student was a senior majoring in history and interested in philosophy as well. Also, he was an unpublished but undaunted poet. He had come to Atlanta from Savannah, his home town, to study for a career as a teacher. He was twenty-three years old and, as he said of himself, he was a black boy with no cream in his coffee.

When he first came to Atlanta, he said he was content to be mildly agnostic without getting into serious arguments about religion. However, after three years he had become specifically anti-Baptist and had had several fist-fights when arguments resulted in loss of tempers.

I didn't start out with any particular reason for disparaging the Baptists. I used to go to a little poor-folks Negro Baptist church down in Savannah and nothing ever happened there to make me mad. There was always plenty of music and singing and not too much preaching and praying. It was a real nice friendly place to go on Sunday and nothing like these society-set Negro Baptist churches here in Atlanta where they act like you're not good enough to walk in and sit down unless you are half-assed whitey-coloured. Down in Savannah there were a lot of mulatto Geechees, but they never went to church and acted like they were any better than black people.

When I came to Atlanta, I couldn't be bothered about going to any church for about a year—Baptist, Methodist, or any denomination. That's the way it was till some people kept after

[240

me to go to one of the big Baptist churches and so I went one Sunday morning.

I wasn't dressed up in elegant haberdashery like the other people and I observed immediately that it was a hell of a big thing for them to put on an ostentatious parade to display their fine clothes for social status or something.

After I'd performed the ritual of scraping the pig shit off the soles of my shoes like we used to do down in Savannah, I entered the doorway of the edifice. Then when I got inside, I asked one of the ushers where I could sit. He was dressed up dandy in a dark-grey silky suit and a white-dotted necktie like he was getting married at a big wedding and posing to get his picture taken for the society page in the newspaper.

He was one of the half-assed whitey-niggers like everybody around there except black-boy me. He looked at my clothes from top to bottom and didn't say a word. I considered myself suitably attired to attend any citified religious service. I had on a pretty good old brown suit and a necktie and a clean white shirt. And I'd shined my shoes that morning just to go to church, too. But he still wouldn't open his mouth and say where I could sit. So I said to hell with him and walked down the aisle and found a seat myself in a pew where there was plenty of space.

Pretty soon two wiggle-rump babes looking twenty-some years old and all doused with perfume came along and sat down in the same pew where I was. They had on flashy diamond rings and all kind of jewelry and were dressed for anybody's party. They had a lot more cream than coffee and their hair was unkinked and fluffed on top of their heads. One of them had dyed red hair and the other one had hers dyed sort of pale brown. Or maybe they were wearing wigs—but that would be hard to tell unless you threw them down and got your hands in it. And you couldn't tell how high priced they were, either, but you could bet it wouldn't be cheap even for old friends.

Soon after they sat down they made a big flutter with their skirts and moved farther away from me. Then they started staring straight at my face like telling me they didn't want a black boy sitting anywhere near them. What I did was stare right back at their pushed-up titties and shake my head like I knew where I could get it a hell of a lot better than that and twice as much for free. When they got the message, that made them a lot madder and they pretended to be insulted.

About that time the big pipe organ started up and the choir people strutted out all dressed in pompous red-and-gold velvet robes. As soon as the singing started, that same supercilious usher tapped me on the shoulder and motioned with a crooking of his finger for me to get up and follow him. I wasn't about to do a goddam thing he told me to do, but I'd had enough of that nauseous atmosphere by that time and needed fresh air. So I got up and walked out.

When I got outside the church, I asked that usher what the hell was the matter. He said I was taking up a seat where some regular members always sat and the church was full that day and there wouldn't be any place for me to sit.

I was going to tell him to hell with his church and walk off if he'd stopped right there and hadn't said something else. What he said was that I didn't look like somebody who'd ever be comfortable in that church and he wouldn't expect to see me there again.

I knew what he was talking about. Maybe it was my old brown suit for one thing. But most of all it was because I'm black with no cream in my coffee.

Man, you should've seen him jump when I called him a half-assed whitey-nigger. Man, how he jumped! You call one of those arrogant bastards a nigger—plain nigger or any other kind—and, man do they jump!

When I called him that, that's when he took a swing at me. But I dodged it. Then I got two or three good shots at his goddam supercilious face with my fists before the other ushers got there

[242

and started kicking at me. They never did any more than kick and back off, because they must've been scared I'd grab one of them and rub his sumptuous silky suit in the dirt. I was mad enough to stay there and beat hell out of them, but there were too many of them by that time and so I just walked off.

I've never been inside a white Baptist church where the people with social pretentiousness congregate and so I don't know what it's like in one of them. But if they're anything like the people who go to that big Negro Baptist church, they probably stage a glamorous exhibition every Sunday morning.

I wouldn't have such a derogatory attitude towards that Negro Baptist church if it wasn't that I went there and saw those stuck-up people with my own eyes. A little religion wouldn't hurt anybody as long as there's plenty of good music and singing along with it. Maybe it would be just the same if those people belonged to some other denomination. But the way it is everybody wants to be high-church Baptist.

All this agitation about passing laws against discrimination—you know, giving Negroes equal rights with whitey and things like that—what the hell! What I want done for me is passing laws to keep Negro Baptist churches and Negro night clubs from discriminating against black-skin people. It's a humiliating experience to be a Negro and have your own people treat you like a leprous outcast the way some of them do.

I'll tell you how it is. There's a certain Negro night club here in Atlanta that does just about the same thing they do at that big Baptist church I went to. I've been in this night club a few times and I know. You go in there like me with a girl to see the show and have a few drinks and they'll make you sit at a table in the back row no matter how many vacant tables they've got up front where the show is. And it won't matter how good-looking and light-skinned the girl is, either. It's my black face they're discriminating against. I might not want to go everywhere whitey goes, but I resent it when my own people humiliate me.

243]

I know why they do it. And they don't mind lying about it, either. Just like the people at that Baptist church, the people who run this night club think they make it classy looking and so goddam élite when they only let half-assed whitey-coloured sit up front where all the bright lights are. They figure those people are the big spenders and belong to the goddam society jet-set and who'd stop coming there if somebody black like me sat close to them at the next table up front.

Another thing is that those people like to have their pictures taken in the night club and put on the society page and don't want a black face to show up in the background. Hell, I don't mind being black. It's me. What I don't like is the discrimination. I want the goddam equal rights, that's all.

And you know the funny thing about that? The two men who own that night club are just as black as I am.

While whitey is passing the laws so Negroes can eat in public restaurants and sleep in public motels, I want him to hurry and pass one to keep Negro night clubs from humiliating me. When I pay my money, I want to go in there and sit at a front-row table to watch the belly dancers. If you can't get a good close point of observation to evaluate the gyratory action, how can you tell if it's worth the money it's costing you?

Five

FROM THE END of the Civil War and into the nineteen-sixties, the era notorious for its hundred-year history of racial discrimination and human injustice, the primary concern of the Southern Negro has been about his social and economic welfare.

Even though there is plentiful evidence of sincere religious faith among the Negro people, for the most part it has been conservative and communal and secondary to the human desire to achieve equality of rights and privileges. Neither the sophistication of the big-city church nor the primitivism of the crossroad mission is representative of Negro religious faith.

For one thing, the Negro in the Deep South has rarely brought into his church the fanatical religious excesses of Anglo-Saxon Protestant fundamentalism. Ramming the head against a wall until dizzy and flailing the body with a stick to produce ecstasy and prodding a rattlesnake to strike with deadly fangs are not ordinary religious spectacles to be seen in a Negro church of any denomination.

The nearest thing to such spectacles is a theatrical exhibition staged by an opportunistic Negro evangelist who calls himself an American Indian or a Hindu or a Muslim and wears exotic headdress as a means of attracting attention. He is the counterpart of the spellbinding white

245]

fundamentalist who earlier in the century would have been equally successful financially staging a medicine show and selling large quantities of cure-all herb tonic to the gullible. As for the people themselves, whether they are sincerely seeking religious inspiration or attending only to satisfy their curiosity, the most appreciated feature of the entertainment is when the audience can take part in the singing of spirituals.

Now in the 'sixties, just as it has been since the first churches were built late in the nineteenth century, Southern Negroes continue to use their churches as a community refuge from the threats and intimidations of dedicated racists among the white citizenry. But this is not all. In addition to the original purpose, in recent years their churches have become the landmarks of a new era—meeting places to organize political protests and demonstrations against the withholding of social, economic, and educational rights.

Since these landmarks are now both real and symbolic, the use of their churches as places to rally to the cause of civil rights has not infrequently resulted in bombing and burning of their buildings by white nightriders in Alabama and Mississippi and elsewhere in the Deep South. In almost every instance, however, these acts of violence are only temporarily intimidating and they eventually serve to inspire Negroes to make greater effort to accomplish their aims.

Just as the former slaves had been excluded long ago from white-church balconies in retaliation for their having gained freedom from slavery, Negroes in the Racial 'Sixties were prohibited by white-ruled school boards in some localities from using their own segregated public schools for civil rights rallies. And so as a consequence the Negro church as a secular gathering place became even more

[246

widely used for the cause of civil rights in a hostile white world.

The leadership in Negro communities throughout this region, now and as it has been for many years past, is almost invariably that of a local Negro minister. In these days, however, he is usually an educated man, calm and capable in judgment, who has the ability to persuade the older generation to put aside its traditional fear of the white man and at the same time restrain the younger generation from engaging in impetuous retaliatory acts.

Such a man might not preach with noteworthy eloquence on Sunday, but during the other days of the week he is most likely to be a fearless and respected leader of his people. And he is likely to be the same man who has been seen many times in the South in recent years leading protest marches along country roads and city streets.

The Deep South Negro of the nineteen-sixties is not necessarily sceptical of the ultimate results of the offered advice and assistance of an outsider who may well be a Northern Negro professionally qualified to aid and direct. Methods of organization are usually helpful, but the execution of such plans might be harmful if not adjusted for the locality.

Since this is where he lives and works, and being aware of the ingrained antagonism of the white racist, the resident Negro can be fearful of his house being burned down. So, understandably, he feels more fortified and secure when the leadership is that of a man who will continue to live side by side with him long after the well-intentioned organizer has come and gone.

As the result of capable leadership and higher education, advantages never known to his father or grandfather, the young Negro of the South today has confidence in himself and in his cause. Among college students and professors in particular, this recently acquired confidence is evident in the unhesitating and straightforward manner with which personal opinions are expressed and controversial matters argued publically.

It would certainly be surprising and probably shocking to Negroes fifty years ago, and of course likewise to many Protestant fundamentalists of today, to hear a Negro college student boldly criticize a policy of the state or federal government or to say that he did not believe in the existence of God. The elder Negroes would probably remain silent with fear while the white fundamentalists would be likely to charge him with being a Communist.

But this is an age of questioning and protest and rejection. And the young Negro of the Deep South is no longer living in isolation; he is breathing the very same invigorating atmosphere of thought and expression that the young white dissident is breathing all over America. These are the same young people who soon will be voting at the polls for their rights as Negro Americans and rejecting any man for public office who fails to honour the full rights of citizenship for all.

After nearly a decade of the Racial 'Sixties, the Negro revolution in the Deep South, which in the early stages was characterized by eat-ins, sit-ins, walk-ins, and similar be-ins, has progressed from excessive physical involvement to being more sophisticated and intellectual in both ambition and activity. When sporadic demonstrations do occur now, they are usually spontaneous and unplanned or they may be instigated by self-seeking proponents.

This advanced phase of the evolution is already fully evident in the college environs of Atlanta and New Orleans and the first indications of it have begun to appear in Birmingham, Jackson, and other Deep South cities.

Even though the traditional Negro minister will continue for a long time to be a mentor and leader, especially in rural communities, in the meanwhile another young generation has come of age and is rapidly revising the political tactics of both Martin Luther King and Stokely Carmichael in urban regions. Civil rights as a cause, having achieved a primary aim, is passing into history and is being supplanted by the intellectually directed causes of social and economic freedom.

The leadership of this emerging movement are the widely-scattered, college-educated, young Negroes—a section of the population to become increasingly larger in number each year—and many of whom are young men who previously would probably have entered the Negro ministry. Now instead many of these people either have become professional educators or have been attracted to the rapidly expanding state and federal government social welfare fields.

This movement of young people into educational and social work has developed from the urbanization of the Deep South Negro during the past decade and the expansion of higher educational opportunities. In the past, the troops recruited by organizers for protests and demonstrations were usually agricultural workers; but, now that mechanized farming has reduced rural job opportunities, the dispossessed have moved to the cities in search of industrial jobs and a better standard of living and there become the troops of the persuasive educators and social welfare workers.

This transition from country to city usually results in leaving behind the guidance of the local Negro minister, as well as the church as a community meeting place, and coming under the influence of the invigorating intellectual atmosphere of the city. If this abrupt move does not end in the social and economic morass of the city slum—which is a constant danger and unavoidable for many—the transition can exhilarate the ambitious younger Negroes and be a relatively easy adjustment for the elder ones.

After all, the Negro church in the Deep South did not originate for the sole purpose of being a temple of religion and in all its history it has been comparable in name only to the white Protestant fundamentalist institutions devoted exclusively to the incestuous practice of religion for religion's sake. And so the born-to-the-city or the former country Negro, urbanized and under the spell of intellectual inquiry and revolt, has little feeling of guilt if he should decide to abandon the church and become an agnostic or atheist.

This is the Negro of the newer generation who is already looking beyond the victories and defeats of the Racial 'Sixties toward the possible achievements and certain perplexities of the next era. Educated and confident in his belief that the massive street demonstrations of the past have served their purpose—and served them well, he is not sure that the same methods of protest would be equally effective in the future.

Instead, this young Negro proposes to appeal to the minds of people in lectures, writings, and conversations to obtain the rights to a more comfortable freedom. He may be a teacher or social worker or, possibly, a minister among his own people. But no matter what his vocation, his influence upon the minds and wills of other Negroes with whom he associates, as well as his appeal to the sympathies of white people, is sure to be reckoned with when votes are counted in the years to come. And in politics and propaganda the word-of-mouth method of influencing people is yet to be found inconsequential.

In the meantime, however, regardless of the aptitudes and accomplishment of the Negro in the Deep South, he is still confronted by the barrier of racial prejudice that makes him a social outcast with little exception in the white world. When tolerated at all, it is usually because he contributes to the cash register of the white-man store and not because he is a member of the college faculty of Tuskeegee or Dillard.

Considering the indignities inflicted upon the Southern Negro in all these years, even aside from the physical tortures, he has given a remarkable performance as a human being and an American citizen. In the course of the amalgamation of the races, it is conceivable that the infusion of such stamina and fortitude eventually will be acknowledged as having provided American civilization with the supremacy and longevity that otherwise it could not have attained.

Whether called the Civil War or the War Between The States or the War Of Northern Aggression Against The South, the eventual result was that while abolishing slavery it gave Negroes only a token of social justice.

The extreme antisocial attitude and prejudice of the white Protestant fundamentalists, the principal evidence of this being law-enforced segregation, discrimination, and disenfranchisement, shackled the greater portion of the Negro population with poverty and illiteracy for more than a half-century after slavery.

The lawmakers of the several Deep South states could

251]

have acted otherwise only if they had not been carriers of infectious racial hatred—a hatred germinated and cultured by perverted principles of Christian religion.

I was very young when my father became so provoked by a political campaign speech by a candidate for state senator that he said he was thinking of resigning from the ministry and entering politics to do his best to defeat such a demagogue and keep him out of public office. But, as before when he said he might leave the ministry, he still did not do so.

What had provoked Ira Sylvester so much was the candidate's campaign promise that if elected he would introduce a bill in the senate to keep the money of white taxpayers from being squandered to provide schooling beyond the fourth grade for Negro children.

The politician had stated in his speech that it was a fact established by eminent theologians that God had purposely limited the Negro to fourth-grade mentality and that it was a waste of tax money, in addition to being against God's will, to provide any additional education for any Negro. Also, he said that Negroes who agitated for education beyond the fourth grade were mulattoes and others of mixed blood and that he would try to get a law passed to prohibit marriage of Negroes of mixed blood so that the race would soon revert to the original blackness that God intended for them to have since the day they were created.

The candidate was defeated in the primary election. And a few days later, perhaps in celebration of the defeat, Ira Sylvester said he was going to Alabama to call on George Washington Carver who he said was living proof that a Negro could be as learned as a white person and, more than that, a genius in science.

When he came back from Alabama, my father said he had two memorable impressions of the visit. One impression was that of having seen George Washington Carver's agricultural research laboratory. The other impression was the result of a speculative discussion about whether it would be good for the breed if the fathering of mulatto children were by white men of superior intellect instead of by white men of inferior intellect as was customary—and, perhaps under certain circumstances, a reversal of the usual white male–Negro female parentage.

Many years later, in the nineteen-sixties, it was startling to realize that I happened to be in the same Alabama town where Ira Sylvester had come to visit George Washington Carver and then to recall what my father had told about their discussion of mulatto parentages.

I was in the company of the calm and genial professor of sociology at the Negro college. He was in his early forties, Southern born with the bronze colouring of the mulatto, and he had been teaching for nearly ten years since receiving his master's degree at a Northern university. In addition to his interest in sociology, he was devoting some of his time to tracing and investigating the origins of the folk music and jazz of the Southern Negro.

I suppose some of the white people of Alabama would be mildly shocked—and some would surely feel that they had been racially affronted—to find out that I am an Episcopalian. You see, in this territory white Episcopalians are looked upon as being high-church untouchables and just a little more privy to God than even Baptists and Methodists. And so you can well imagine what the local reaction might be if I declared myself publically. How presumptuous can a Negro get!

All good niggers, as they say in Alabama, had better by God be nigger Baptists—or else. Well, I'm one of those mindful that the or-else threat is real and can result in spiteful acts against us. But I don't think a happening is likely, anyhow, because I don't plan to tempt fate in a part of the country where I would provoke the lords of segregation by sitting in the same church with white people. As it is, when I do attend the church of my choice, which is possible only two or three times a year during a summer vacation, it usually takes place in New York or Philadelphia.

There is good reason why I'm an Episcopalian—otherwise by now I'd certainly be an agnostic or an out-and-out atheist. The reason for my being what I am is in honour of my parentage. I'll tell you about that in a few minutes.

But to start with, you can see that both my wife and I have mixed racial blood. Like her, I'm mulatto both in appearance and in fact—half white, half black—and damn proud of it, too. This gives me a constant pull in two directions—a double allegiance —and it's such a good feeling that I've never wanted to disavow my allegiance to either side of me.

One result of this dual allegiance is that I accept the condition that I'm to be classified as Negro upon sight wherever I go in the United States and I'm content to live with that condition all my life. And because I honour my heritage I can be tolerant and unresentful of any racial affront and not be hateful of all things white and all things black.

This attitude of mine is not the result of calculated delusion or self-hypnosis. I consider myself fortunate for being the offspring of the accident of birth—or in my case perhaps the design of birth—because this gives me the advantage of being able to appreciate and have a subjective feeling for each race of which I'm a part.

So far so good. But now we come to that point where we are faced by that inevitable human frailty—prejudice. White, black, or mixed, we all have it to some degree and I'm no different in that

[254

respect than the next human being to come along. However, since I know I'm firmly lodged in the ethnic category of mulatto, I think my personal prejudice is justified and logical. And it's not because I think I'm better than the white man or the black man. Or feel that I'm inferior to either. It's because of unusual parentage—unusual that is, for a Deep South mulatto.

I've been trying to lead up to an explanation of why I'm a prejudiced man and now I'll tell you what my prejudice is.

I dislike, disapprove, disagree, disavow, and in every other way have a dissenting attitude toward what I consider the vainglorious aims of so-called Black Power. Black Power or Black Muslim, or any other similar name—these are terms that imply that only a person with a black-black skin is eligible to represent the Negro. I've been a Negro long enough to know better than that.

And even if my feelings about Black Power—which I consider to be only an opportunistic, political, updated-counterpart of the discredited religious concept of the Black Bible, Black Moses, Black Jesus, Black Virgin Mary—well I'd better stop right here and cool off about that. Let's just say the professional blacks have as much claim to their fantasy as the atavistic Southern white racists have to their fantasy.

Now, after that outburst, what I want to say is that I'll continue going my way and taking pride in being the mulatto that I am—which is my method of expressing gratitude for, and honouring, my parents.

As you can see, this is something I'm deeply sentimental about. And for reason. Because my mother was a white woman. That's right. A white woman. And nobody could be any more white than she was. A blonde-haired, blue-eyed, Anglo-Saxon, English woman—and as dear and devoted a mother any child could have in this world.

Now, that will explain why I'm an Episcopalian—she was a faithful member of the Episcopal church.

255]

It all began more than forty years ago in Mobile where my mother was a hospital nurse. She had come to this country as a young girl for the adventure of it—just as many adventurous English people have done.

My father was a black man, a Bahaman or West Indian, which ever, and he met my mother in Mobile. He was a seaman on a freighter and his ship did not come back to Mobile again. I never saw him. But I revere him for being my father. He is the other half of me.

My mother could have abandoned me—there were many ways she could have got rid of me. Adoption by a Negro family. An orphanage. And so on. But she was not that kind of mother. She kept me and she raised me in that narrow zone of borderland between white and Negro in Mobile and other Southern cities. It's a hazy zone without established rights of residence for either race that can be block wide in one place, several blocks wide at another, and the only place where a physical merging of the races is outlawed but tolerated. It's like walking in a dense fog at night and not knowing exactly where you are and being fearful of your next step.

Of course I had no understanding at all then of how difficult life was for my mother—a white woman in the South living in that dim twilight zone of two worlds and working to raise and educate a Negro child. But she was determined that I was to get an education. And she succeeded, too, God bless her. Working to support me for those many years, she got me into my education and she kept it up until I was old enough to go to work and support myself in high school and college.

I didn't see my mother very often during the last years of her life. In a place like Mobile—she preferred living there because it had been her home for most of her life—and in Mobile it would not have been good for either of us if a Negro man had frequently been seen visiting a white woman. When I did go to see her after she had moved to the white residential part of town, it was always

[256

dark and both of us felt more secure when it was a rainy night with few people—white people—on the street.

And even nowadays when I visit her grave in the white cemetery in Mobile, I'm always careful of my timing and then hurry to avoid a challenge by somebody to explain why a Negro man would be placing flowers on the grave of a white woman.

Maybe after all I do consider myself as being just a little bit fortunate. Not conceited. Not superior. Only fortunate. And if there is any justification for feeling like I do, it's because I know how fortunate it is to be a Southern Negro who had a loving, white, church-going Episcopalian mother who devoted herself to helping her mulatto son get an education so he could rise above what for most of us is a devastating life in our part of the world.